THE CO   Е
CHINESE COOKBOOK

1000 Days of Simple and Delicious Traditional and Modern Recipes for

Chinese Cuisine Lovers

PARK HOU

Table of Contents

Introduction

Finding a cookbook that fits your needs and desires is no easy task. In today's age of information bombardment, people get swarmed with commercials for different products every day. We read ads for diets and cookbooks, and they all promise that their method is revolutionary and will answer all your heart's desires. Because of this oversaturation, it is essential to sit back, relax, and go back to the classics. Chinese food is known for its incredible taste, healthy, fresh ingredients, and positive impact on our bodies.

Few things stir the imagination as much as the sound of Chinese food sizzling in a wok! The images, tastes, and smells associated with Chinese food have been a culinary world staple for centuries. Chinese food is usually light but rich in flavors. One can often find rice and rice noodles, vegetables, pork, chicken, seafood, and an array of oriental spices in Chinese dishes. Still, the extensive variation in potential flavors never ceases to amaze and delight the cook, and the people blessed to be tasting these delights.

Sometimes we don't need to try cutting-edge, new ways of consuming food; we need to adopt the good habits we humans have been doing for thousands of years. Chinese food has vegetables, lean protein sources, and spices that make it all come together and is usually cooked in delicious ways but won't add weight to the scale.

Chapter 1
Basics of Chinese Food

History of Chinese Food

Chinese cuisine dates back millennia and is the cornerstone of one of the first civilizations on Earth. It grew in conjunction with Chinese culture as a whole and with traditional Chinese medicine, which often focuses on herbs, healthy plants, and beneficial eating habits. Millenniums of evolution made Chinese cuisine versatile and unique. As the cultures blended on the Asian continent, Chinese food adopted bits and pieces and continued to grow, striving toward excellence with each passing century.

As we can see in every facet of our culture, Chinese cuisine is now a staple of our world, as much as it has been since immemorial. Whenever we watch a movie nowadays, it is a common occurrence to have the characters order Chinese food. We would be hard-pressed to find a person who hasn't tried Chinese food in at least some form. Naturally, like any other food, the best kind of Chinese food is the one you cook at home, with quality ingredients and the time and care that you invest in a dish.

Besides exquisite tastes, health is a huge reason many incorporate Chinese cuisine into their lives. Steamed vegetables and easy-to-digest lean protein sources are the staples of Chinese food. Nutritional properties of Chinese food help with many unfavorable human conditions, including heart disease and diabetes, as well as weight loss. Many have successfully embarked on a life-changing weight loss journey by eating more Chinese food. By doing this, you will naturally start eating more vegetables and more clean, lean proteins, and the beneficial effects on your mind and body will be instantly visible. Not only will your waist become narrower, but you will also have more energy throughout the day and adopt a more positive outlook on life.

You will, however, need to learn recipes before you set out on your own and become a master Chinese food chef. That might seem daunting at first but fear not because all you need to start learning how to become a master of Chinese cooking is this cookbook! We have compiled a list of recipes for everyone, from experienced master chefs to novice Chinese cuisine enthusiasts who seldom pick up a wok.

Whether you want to lose weight, start eating healthier, or are simply in the mood for experimenting a bit and adding new dishes to your everyday routine, this cookbook will suit your needs perfectly. If you are a novice cook on the path of culinary skills improvement, following the recipes word by word will enable you to gain the skills necessary for improvement and, eventually, for improvisation and crafting your signature dishes. Everything, from ingredients to cooking methods, is laid out in an easy-to-follow format, and the more you use the recipes from this cookbook, the handier you will become with Chinese cooking.

Ingredients in Chinese cuisine are usually steamed and seared, rarely fried, so the final product's nutritious values are kept intact. Light in calories but rich in flavors, Chinese food will keep you fit and full!

Once the cook follows the recipes in this cookbook enough, it will become easy to combine and incorporate substitutes into dishes and, in time, fine-tune the meals according to personal preferences. Try following the recipes closely the first time you make a dish, then combine and add/reduce a few ingredients the second time you decide to cook that dish. Often it is enough to replace the type of vegetable, a particular spice, or a source of protein in a recipe to get a new take on a tried-and-true formula! Much like a musician first must learn chords and basics to improvise, you too can use this cookbook to gain a grip on Chinese cooking to become a true master. There's beauty in improvisation, and you will become a Master of It when you learn the basics with this cookbook!

Variations in Chinese dishes mean that by reading this cookbook, you will learn to make soups, such as the famous egg-drop soup or the hot and sour soup, salads, bamboo, and veggie stir fries, sauces, and more. Light, easy-to-cook meals are present, but if you'd like to impress your friends with a colorful feast with entrees, main dishes, soups, dips, and sauces (and yes, even desserts!) Chinese cuisine will have an answer for you. There are recipes for quick, easy-to-make snacks, too, and they can serve as a great alternative to the usual sodium-filled finger food one can usually find in supermarkets and stores. Soon enough, you will become a master at crafting exquisite meals filled with nutritional properties and rich flavors.

Equip Yourself with Varied Chinese Meal Materials

Stocking your cupboard with quality ingredients is crucial when cooking Chinese dishes. While you can use much of what's in your closet right now, equipping yourself with new, Chinese food-specific herbs, spices, and sauces can only add extra flavor to your dishes. Let's look at a few ingredients that give Chinese food its recognizable flavor, texture, and soul.

1.   Different Kinds of Soy Sauce

For most people, soy sauce is the first thing that comes to mind regarding Chinese food. Still, it is not widely known that there are multiple soy sauces. Light soy sauce contains more salt than its dark counterpart. Because of this property, light soy sauce is usually used for dipping and sometimes for seasoning. Dark soy sauce is less salty but has a more robust flavor. Where pro cooks add light soy sauce at the end of the cooking process, dark soy sauce is usually used for cooking because heat helps bring out its solid molasses and caramel-like flavors.

2.   Other Sauces and Dips

While soy sauce is vital to Chinese cuisine, cooks will often use a variety of other spices and dips too. Chili bean sauce is thicker than soy sauce and is used in dishes that require a dash of spiciness and hotness. It is made from chilies and fermented beans, and different sauce masters add various spices. This spicy condiment is often found in the southwestern parts of China. Oyster sauce has a specific taste that's unlike any other. Chefs use it to add a caramel-like, umami flavor to their dishes. It usually boasts a rich, savory taste and a dense texture, making the food filling and rich. Sesame oil is rarely recognized by name but feels instantly familiar when we put a drop of it on our tongues. Its nutty taste makes it a versatile addition to different vegetable dishes, dips, salads, and many other food groups. Rice wine: much like Western cuisine, Chinese food uses wine not only for drinking but for cooking too. The most famous wine in Chinese cuisine is Shaoxing rice wine, and pro chefs use just a little bit of it when it is added to dishes.

3.   Spices

Spices can make or break a dish. Like in Western cuisine, salt and pepper are the basics of Chinese dishes. One important distinction is that instead of black peppers, Chinese food often uses Sichuan pepper. While they look almost the same, Sichuan peppercorns provide a different distinct flavor that will make your Chinese dishes stand out among the rest. It is important to buy whole peppercorns; if you can find them, grind them up, mix them with chili, and you are good to go. Shiitake mushrooms are an ingredient but can be used as a spice too. A creative way to introduce flavors into your dishes is to dry the mushroom, infuse them with liquids, and add them to a plate or a broth. Five Spice Powder is made from Sichuan peppercorns, cloves, cinnamon, star anise, and fennel. Brown powder is the main ingredient of many Chinese dishes. Ginger and turmeric are healthy roots that can be added to Chinese food and beverages for multiple health benefits. They also have an enjoyable, spicy, and fresh taste that can add a nice dimension to the food you are preparing. Chinese vinegar is a spicy, sometimes sweet, or pungent alternative to vinegar found in Western cuisine. It is usually made from rice.

4.   Rice

It is impossible to talk about Chinese food without mentioning rice. There are multiple kinds of rice, though, and the choice between them can be crucial to the success of your dish. Jasmine rice is subtle, soft, sweet, and delicate. Use it for light foods, for a variety of fish-based meals, for easy stir-fries, and as a side dish to heartier meat plates. Basmati rice is a versatile all-rounder. If you want to get just one type of rice and use it in all the meals, Basmati is a solid choice. It has a more pungent taste than Jasmine rice and works well with meats, hearty sauces, and as part of the main course. Japonica rice is sticky, tiny, and round. The most common use for this kind of rice is stuffing vegetables because it binds well. You can also use it for dumplings and desserts. Brown rice is the less processed equivalent of white rice. If you want to implement as many healthy options as possible in your diet, substitute regular rice for brown rice, and you will consume more fiber, minerals, and vitamins.

5.   Vegetables

Black beans are one of the most used vegetables in Chinese cuisine. They are a variety of soya beans and are usually fermented before use. Chilies, whether dried or fresh, are often added to many Chinese dishes. The spice they provide is indispensable, and capsaicin, an ingredient that gives chili peppers their signature taste, has many health benefits. Spring onions can be put in seasoning oils, added to stir-fries, and eaten fresh as an addition to almost any food. Shallots are mild-flavored onions that are great, both fried and fresh.

6.   Protein

Chinese food uses many sources of protein. You can find egg recipes in this cookbook and learn to make dishes like Egg Foo Young or Chinese eggrolls. Chicken is a top-rated protein source in Chinese cuisine. The most famous chicken recipe is Kung Pao Chicken, a legendary dish that will undoubtedly become a favorite of you and your family. If you are interested in something a bit heartier, try some beef recipes. Sesame Beef is a favorite of millions and is a perfect recipe you can master quickly. Pork is used widely too, and once you master various ways to cook meat in Chinese style, you can make classics like Red Braised Pork or Twice-Cooked Pork. Seafood plays a huge part, too, and can often be a basis for some of the most interesting Chinese recipes.

7.   Noodles

While rice is synonymous with Chinese cuisine, noodles play a massive part in it too. Like all other food groups used in Chinese cuisine, noodles come in various forms. Egg noodles, or Chow Mein, are versatile and easy to cook because they rarely stick to the pan. Udon noodles are thick and can be found in soups and fried dishes. Unlike Udon noodles, Vermicelli noodles are thin and must be cooked carefully because they are known for sticking to the pan. Ho Fun noodles are flat and thick and usually accompany beef-based recipes.

Chapter 2
Start your Chinese Food Journey

As you can see from the list of ingredients, Chinese food is heaven for everyone who enjoys versatility and creativity. The many elements mean that you can mix and match to your heart's desire and add your twists to tried-and-true recipes. Besides the cornucopia of ingredients that Chinese cuisine uses, there are just as many ways to cook those ingredients. These various cooking methods provide unique takes on processing the elements, and every single one gives a specific particular benefit to the final dish.

Various Chinese Cooking Styles

1.   Stir-Fry

Probably the most known cooking method in Chinese cuisine is stir-frying. It is quick, delicious, simple, and uses the trademark Chinese wok. The heat should be high, and vegetables and other ingredients should spend just a little bit of time on the wok. Since we use just a touch of oil when we stir-fry, this method is also incredibly healthy and beneficial to weight loss.

2.   Braising

Braising usually takes longer than stir-frying, but the result is always spectacular. To braise, we must use a little broth and boil the ingredients at high temperatures. Once we are done with boiling, simmer the ingredients at low heat for hours. Beef with potatoes, and chicken with mushrooms, are best prepared by braising.

3.   Steaming

Widely recognized to be the healthiest way to cook food, steaming was invented in China. Initially, it was used to steam dumplings but has since evolved to include steamed veggies, buns, and certain types of fish. When we steam food, it doesn't lose any nutritional properties because the water does not touch the ingredients. Steaming food can take a long time, but the results are both tasty and healthy.

4.   Boiling

Boiling is considered the simplest way to cook food, but that doesn't mean it has to be boring. When we boil, we cut the ingredients and place them in piping-hot water. This method is usually used to create soups and stews. Some of the favorite soups in Chinese cuisine are Lotus Root and Pork soup, Fish and Tofu soup, Ching Po Leung Cantonese Herb soup, and many more.

Plenty of Other Cooking Options

This is not a complete list of ways we can cook food. Many receipts call for roasting, deep-frying, or cold-soaking ingredients to create dishes. Sometimes, a final dish will contain raw ingredients in combination with cooked ones. Most dishes are made by combining different cooking methods and knowing how to do that is one of the trademark secrets that you will discover by reading through this cookbook.

By now, you understand the ingredients and ways to cook Chinese food. Once you read this cookbook, you will be fully equipped to follow through on some recipes and take the first step toward becoming a Chinese food master chef! Regularly eating Chinese food will bring many benefits to your life. Of course, the most essential property of any food is health.

Because soups are such an essential part of Chinese cuisine, people tend to eat less. Chinese soups are not thick or filled with fats but remain rich in flavors, so a person feels full without indulging in too many calories. Soups are eaten slowly, too, so our stomach has the time to send signals of satiety to the brain, and we end up not overeating. Not to mention how no meal is complete until we've had our fill of delicious, savory soup. Tofu is especially nice in combination with one of many Chinese soups.

If you decide to go the extra mile and decide to eat with chopsticks when you switch from soup to the main dish, the benefits of eating slowly will be even more effective. Chopsticks make you eat smaller bites slower, which is proven beneficial for weight loss because we end up feeling full quicker, preventing us from overeating food.

Since Chinese cuisine uses many vegetables, it is highly effective in balancing carbs. You are perfectly safe to eat white rice with your dishes because there will be a lot of vegetables, so everything will turn out perfectly balanced. Since Chinese cooking is versatile, you can use brown rice instead of white if you want to go the extra mile regarding health.

If you look at recipes in this cookbook, you will notice that not many contain milk and milk-based products. Cow milk has been proven to be unhealthy for human use time and time again, and it causes numerous allergic reactions as well as digestive issues.

Oils can be the most troublesome part of any diet since they are widely considered unhealthy, filled with calories, and fatty. However, the most popular type of oil in China is sesame oil, which is rich in monounsaturated and polyunsaturated fatty acids. There are different kinds of fats, and sesame oil contains healthy fats, which will lessen the risks of type 2 diabetes, stroke, high blood pressure, and weight gain. Chinese food also uses a small amount of oil in most dishes, lessening the number of calories in the final product.

When we look at obesity statistics, it is noticeable that China is almost always near the bottom of the chart. The recipes in this cookbook contain the dishes that Chinese people eat to stay healthy while enjoying the many flavors their cuisine has to offer. Balance is a massive part of Chinese culture, and it is reflected in Chinese food as well. That's why almost no dishes contain only meat or only rice; everything is blended in perfect proportions to provide a healthy, nutritious, and flavorful final product.

Steamed Seitan

Prep time: 10 minutes, plus 2 hours 15 minutes to 3 hours 15 minutes to rest|Cook time: 40 minutes|Makes About 12 Ounces (350g)

- ⅔ cup warm water
- ¼ teaspoon active dry yeast
- ¼ teaspoon granulated sugar
- 1 cup vital wheat gluten
- SPECIAL EQUIPMENT:
- Flat-bottomed stainless steel or bamboo steamer with a large pot

1. In a medium bowl, mix the water, yeast, and sugar. Let it rest for 15 minutes.
2. Add the wheat gluten gradually while stirring quickly with chopsticks to form lumps. If there is still dry flour left, add a little more water. Be careful not to add too much water.
3. Knead the dough for 2 minutes on a flat surface. Stretch the dough into a flat round shape and spread it on a piece of parchment paper. Press the dough to ¾ inch thick. Cover it with a damp kitchen towel to keep moist. Let it rise on the counter for 2 to 3 hours, until the dough has doubled in size.
4. Lift the parchment paper and transfer the dough to the dish you will use in the steamer or directly into the steamer basket.
5. Heat the steamer over high heat until it comes to a full steam. Reduce the heat to medium and steam for 30 minutes. Remove the seitan from the steamer. Use a pair of scissors to cut the seitan into 1-inch cubes.
6. Store the seitan in an airtight container in the refrigerator for 2 days or in the freezer for up to 1 month.

Fried Gluten Balls

Prep time: 5 minutes, plus 1½ hours to rest|Cook time: 40 minutes| makes about 27 balls (6½ oz / 180g)

- 1¼ cups water
- ½ teaspoon sea salt
- ¾ cup vital wheat gluten
- Canola oil, for deep-frying

1. Pour the water into a medium bowl. In a small bowl, mix together the salt and wheat gluten. Sprinkle the wheat gluten mixture into the bowl of water while stirring quickly with chopsticks. Gently massage the dough for 2 minutes in the water until all the gluten flour sticks together, then squeeze out the extra water from the dough. Do not knead. Discard the starchy water.
2. Gently pull the dough into small, round cherry-size pieces. Let them rest on a plate for 1½ hours to relax the gluten.
3. In a deep pot, heat at least 3 inches deep of oil over medium-low heat. When the surface of the oil begins moving slowly (250° to 280°F), carefully add a few of the gluten pieces, not overcrowding the pot, and fry them for 7 to 10 minutes. Using chopsticks to keep them from sticking and the back of a spider strainer or slotted spoon to submerge them in the oil, turn the pieces frequently until they are light yellow and about the size of a plum. Remove the balls using the spider strainer and repeat with the remaining dough.
4. The gluten balls will deflate once cooled. Immediately return them to the oil and fry them again for 2 minutes over medium heat (325° to 350°F). They will expand again and hold their shape once thoroughly cooked. The finished gluten balls should be light golden.
5. Freeze the balls in an airtight container or zip-top bags for up to 3 months.

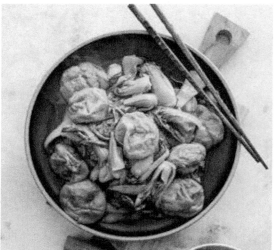

Homemade Soy Milk

Prep time: 1 hour, plus 12 to 48 hours to soak|Cook time: 25 minutes| Makes 8 cups

- 1 pound (454g) dried soybeans
- 10 cups water
- SPECIAL EQUIPMENT:
- Nut milk bag

1. In a large bowl, soak the soybeans in enough water to generously cover for a minimum of 12 hours and up to 2 days. Change the water every 8 to 12 hours. Make sure the soybeans are completely submerged. Drain and rinse the soybeans.
2. Working in batches, combine the soaked soybeans and the water and puree. Pour the soybean puree into a nut milk bag held over a large pot. Squeeze out as much soy milk as possible into the pot. Discard or repurpose the soy pulp.
3. Bring the pot of soy milk to a boil over high heat, uncovered. Keep a careful eye on the soy milk as it can easily boil over. Once the soy milk comes to a boil, keep it at a constantly boiling temperature without overflowing (around medium heat) for 15 to 20 minutes, stirring frequently.
4. Use a fine-mesh skimmer to remove any foam from the top of the soy milk. Remove the pot from the heat. Store the soy milk in a sealed jar in the refrigerator for up to 1 week.

Tofu From Scratch

Prep time: 25 minutes, plus time to press|Cook time: 10 minutes| Makes 1 block (of varying weights)

- 8 cups Homemade Soy Milk or store-bought soy milk
- 1 tablespoon gypsum (calcium sulfate)
- 2 cups water

SPECIAL EQUIPMENT:
- Tofu press and cheesecloth

1. In a large pot, bring the soy milk to a boil. Remove from the heat immediately.
2. In a small bowl, dilute the gypsum in the water. Pour the solution into the soy milk. Stir quickly, then let the soy milk sit for 3 to 5 minutes, until curds form and the liquid turns clear.
3. Line a tofu press with cheesecloth. Place the tofu press on a stand over a bowl. Ladle the tofu curds into the mold and smooth them gently with your fingers to fill in the space. Fold the cheesecloth over to wrap the tofu. Place the tofu press cover on top of the tofu.
4. For extra-firm tofu: Place a 4-pound weight on the tofu and press for 20 minutes. For firm tofu: Use a 3-pound weight for 15 minutes. For medium-firm tofu: Use a 2-pound weight for 10 minutes. For soft tofu: Use a 1-pound weight for 5 minutes.
5. Let the tofu cool and store in cold water in an airtight container in the refrigerator, changing the water every day, for up to 5 days.

Tofu Puffs

Prep time: 5 minutes|Cook time: 30 minutes|Makes 12 tofu puffs

- ⅔ block extra-firm Tofu from Scratch or 1 (16oz / 454g) package store-bought extra-firm tofu
- 1 teaspoon sea salt
- 1 cup water
- Canola oil, for deep-frying

1. Cut the tofu into 1- to 1½-inch cubes.
2. In a small bowl, dissolve the salt in the water. Dip the tofu in the salt water, then pat it dry.
3. In a deep pot, heat at least 3 inches of oil over medium-low heat. When the surface of the oil begins moving slowly (250° to 280°F), working in batches, carefully place the tofu cubes into the oil, not overcrowding the pot. Fry for 8 to 10 minutes, until they float. Be patient with frying at low temperatures; if the heat is too high, it will overcook and harden the tofu's surface.
4. Increase the heat to medium-high. Continue frying the tofu for 2 to 3 minutes, until the surface turns a light golden color but is still soft. Remove the tofu using a spider strainer or a slotted spoon.
5. Freeze the tofu puffs in an airtight container or zip-top bag for up to 1 month.

Mock Meat

Prep time: 10 minutes, plus 20 minutes to rest|Cook time: 25 minutes|Serves 4

- 1 (11oz / 320g) package fresh bean curd sheets
- 4 cups water
- 3 tablespoons Shaoxing wine
- 2 tablespoons Chinese light soy sauce
- 2 teaspoons sea salt
- 1 teaspoon five-spice powder
- ½ teaspoon baking soda

1. Cut the bean curd sheets into strips 2 inches long and ½ inch wide.
2. In a medium pot, combine the water, rice wine, soy sauce, salt, five-spice powder, and baking soda. Add the bean curd strips. Bring the pot to a boil over high heat, then reduce the heat to medium-low. Cover the pot and simmer for 15 minutes, or until the bean curd strips are very soft. (The time may vary slightly depending on the brand of your bean curd.) Thoroughly drain the bean curd strips in a colander.
3. Lay a double layer of 18-inch square cheesecloth on the cutting board. Place the bean curd strips in the middle, then roll them into a log. Wrap the cheesecloth tightly around the bean curd roll. Place a flat heavy object on top, such as a cast-iron skillet. Press the bean curd roll for 20 minutes.
4. Unwrap the cheesecloth. Cut the mock meat into slices to serve. If you're not eating it right away, store the mock meat log in an airtight container in the refrigerator for up to 3 days.

Sichuan Chili Oil

Prep time: 5 minutes | Cook time: 5 minutes | Makes 2 cups

- ⅓ cup coarse chili pepper powder
- ¼ cup fine chili pepper powder
- 2 tablespoons white sesame seeds
- 1 teaspoon sea salt
- ½ teaspoon five-spice powder
- 2 cups canola oil
- 1 tablespoon black vinegar

1. In a large heatproof bowl, combine both chili pepper powders, the sesame seeds, the salt, and the five-spice powder.
2. In a saucepan, heat the oil over medium-high heat until it just begins to smoke. Remove the pan from the heat and let it cool off for a minute, until the oil is no longer at its smoke point but still sizzles immediately when a wooden chopstick is put in it (it should be around 380°F).
3. Pour half of the hot oil over the chili pepper mix. It will sizzle. Stir immediately to combine the oil and chili pepper powder. Let the mixture sit for 1 minute, then add the black vinegar for extra aroma. Pour the other half of the hot oil into the mixture. It should sizzle more violently this time. Stir again.
4. Store the chili oil in a sealed glass jar in the pantry for up to 2 months.

Dumpling Dipping Sauce

Prep time: 5 minutes | Cook time: 5 minutes | Serves 4

- ¼ cup black vinegar
- 6 garlic cloves, finely minced
- 2 tablespoons Chinese light soy sauce
- 2 teaspoons sesame oil
- 1 teaspoon granulated sugar

1. In a small bowl, combine the black vinegar, garlic, soy sauce, sesame oil, and sugar.
2. Mix all the ingredients together until well combined. Serve fresh.

Mock Meat Dipping Sauce

Prep time: 5 minutes | Cook time: 5 minutes | Serves 4

- 2 tablespoons finely chopped fresh cilantro
- 1 tablespoon finely minced fresh ginger
- Pinch five-spice powder
- 2 tablespoons canola oil
- 2 tablespoons Chinese light soy sauce
- ½ teaspoon granulated sugar

1. In a small heatproof bowl, combine the cilantro, ginger, and five-spice powder.
2. In a skillet or a wok, heat the oil over high heat until it begins to smoke. Immediately pour the hot oil onto the ginger and cilantro. The sizzling oil will release the aroma from the herbs and spices.
3. Add the soy sauce and sugar to the bowl. Stir to combine with a spoon. Serve fresh.

Tofu Puddings In Ginger-Sugar Syrup

Prep time: 10 minutes, plus 10 minutes to rest | Cook time: 35 minutes | Serves 6

- 3 cups water, plus 6 tablespoons
- 1 cup packed light brown sugar
- ⅓ cup thinly sliced fresh ginger
- 3 tablespoons cornstarch
- 3 teaspoons gypsum (calcium sulfate)
- 8 cups Homemade Soy Milk or store-bought soy milk

1. In a small pot, combine 3 cups of water, the brown sugar, and ginger. Bring the mixture to a boil over high heat. Reduce the heat to medium-low, cover the pot, and simmer for 20 minutes.
2. Meanwhile, in each of six bowls, mix together 1½ teaspoons of cornstarch, ½ teaspoon of gypsum, and 1 tablespoon of water.
3. In a large pot, bring the soy milk to a full boil, then immediately remove it from the heat. Pour 1⅓ cups of the hot soy milk into each bowl from a high position with a fast pour, using the force of the liquid to quickly disperse the gypsum. Do not stir. Let the bowls sit undisturbed for 10 minutes, or until the soy milk turns into a pudding. Use a spoon to carefully remove any tofu skin and foam from the surface.
4. Strain the ginger syrup through a fine-mesh sieve (discard the ginger).
5. Serve both the pudding and the syrup either hot or cold. For a cold dessert, keep the pudding and the syrup chilled in the refrigerator. When ready to serve, pour the ginger-sugar syrup to taste over the puddings.

Mung Bean Cakes

Prep time: 15 minutes, plus 12 hours to soak | Cook time: 50 minutes | Serves 6

- 1½ cups peeled dried mung beans
- 1 cup granulated sugar
- ½ cup corn oil, or another very mild-flavored oil
- SPECIAL EQUIPMENT:
- Flat-bottomed stainless steel or bamboo steamer with a large pot
- Moon cake mold

1. Soak the beans for 12 hours or overnight. Drain them completely.
2. Place the beans on a deep plate in a steamer. Heat the steamer over high heat until it comes to full steam. Reduce the heat to medium and steam for 30 minutes. Press a bean between your fingers; if it crumbles, it's cooked.
3. Transfer the beans to a food processor and pulse to break them down into a powder. Transfer to a large bowl. Stir in the sugar and the oil and mix well.
4. Heat a wok or a large nonstick skillet over medium heat. Add the paste to the wok and cook it to dry up excess moisture and dissolve the sugar. Fold it with a spatula constantly to prevent browning, until the paste turns into a dough.
5. Let the dough cool for about 10 minutes. Press a piece of the dough into a moon cake mold to make a small cake (follow the instructions that came with the mold as they can differ in size). Repeat until all of the dough has been used. (If you don't have a moon cake mold, you can use the cups of a silicone baking mold. Or instead of making individual cakes, press the dough into a container to form a block and then cut it into squares.)
6. Serve the cakes either fresh or chilled for a better taste. If you're not eating them right away, store in an airtight container in the refrigerator for up to 3 days.

Chili Oil

Prep time: 5 minutes | Cook time: 45 minutes| Makes over a quart of chili oil

- 5 cups vegetable oil
- ½ cup sesame oil
- 4 cups whole dried chilies, slightly crushed
- ½ cup Sichuan peppercorns
- 4 cloves garlic, peeled and crushed
- 1 finger ginger, peeled and chopped
- 1 piece star anise
- 1 tablespoon kosher salt
- ½ tablespoon MSG

1. Mix the vegetable oil and sesame oil in saucepan on medium heat until you see one whiff of smoke.
2. While you are carefully watching the oil come up to temperature, mix the chilies, peppercorns, garlic, ginger, star anise, and salt in a large metal mixing bowl.
3. When the oil is ready, pour into the bowl, submerging all the chilies and aromatics. (Be careful. Make sure there is no water in the bowl or on the aromatics or the oil will splatter. Not kidding, this can be a dangerous step. You have to respect hot oil.)
4. Let it sit for 30 minutes and cool down. Add the MSG.
5. Strain out the aromatics the next day, or let it sit on the bottom to develop even more flavor with a little time.

Black Sesame Rice Balls

Prep time: 50 minutes | Cook time: 15 minutes| Serves 6

- ½ cup toasted black sesame seeds
- 3 tablespoons granulated sugar
- 3 tablespoons coconut oil
- 1½ cups glutinous rice flour
- ⅓ cup hot water
- ¼ cup room-temperature water (or less)

1. In a high-powered blender, combine the sesame seeds and sugar and process until the oil from the sesame seeds binds with the sugar and turns into a thick paste. Transfer the mixture to a bowl and mix in the coconut oil.
2. Pour the mixture into a zip-top bag and shape it into a rectangular block ½ inch thick. Chill it in the freezer for 20 minutes, or until just hardened.
3. Meanwhile, place the glutinous rice flour in a small bowl and gradually pour the hot water into it, stirring with a pair of chopsticks. Add the room-temperature water to the bowl a little at a time, using your hands to mix everything together. Stop adding water when the dough is very soft. Knead the dough until smooth. Let it rest for 10 minutes.
4. Remove the sesame filling from the freezer. Cut it into 32 equal pieces. Roll each piece into a ball. Place the balls on a plate and freeze them for 15 minutes, or until they are completely frozen.
5. Divide the dough into 32 equal pieces. Press a piece into a bowl shape. Place a piece of frozen sesame filling inside, then seal the rice flour wrapper to enclose the filling. Roll the ball between your palms to smooth it. Repeat with the remaining balls.
6. Bring a pot of water to a boil. Working in batches, drop some rice balls into the water and cook for 3 to 4 minutes, stirring, until they float to the surface. Repeat until all the rice balls are cooked. Serve hot with some of the cooking liquid.

Candyfloss Sweet Potato

Prep time: 5 minutes | Cook time: 25 minutes| Serves 4

- 4 medium sweet potatoes (1lb /454g)
- 3 tablespoons cornstarch
- 1 tablespoon canola oil, plus more for deep-frying
- ½ cup granulated sugar
- ¼ cup water
- 1 tablespoon distilled white vinegar

1. Peel and quarter the sweet potatoes lengthwise. Roll-cut them (see here) to form irregular bite-size pieces. Bring a medium pot of water to a boil over high heat. Drop the sweet potato into the water and cook them for 3 minutes. Drain the pieces of sweet potato in a colander.
2. In a large bowl, toss the pieces of sweet potato in the cornstarch.
3. In a deep pot, heat at least 3 inches of oil over medium heat. When a wooden chopstick lowered into the oil immediately sizzles (350°F), the oil is ready. Add the pieces of sweet potato and fry them for 5 minutes. Remove them with a spider strainer or slotted spoon.
4. In a wok or large skillet, heat the sugar, water, and 1 tablespoon of oil over medium heat. Continue stirring for 6 to 8 minutes, until the sugar has reduced to a golden syrup. Add the white vinegar, then add sweet potato. Flip everything for a few seconds to coat the sweet potato evenly. Transfer them to a plate immediately.
5. Eat this dish right away before the sugar coating hardens.

Amber Walnuts

Prep time: 5 minutes | Cook time: 25 minutes| Serves 4

- 2 cups walnuts
- ½ cup granulated sugar
- ⅛ teaspoon sea salt
- ⅓ cup water
- 1½ cups canola oil
- 2 tablespoons toasted white sesame seeds

1. Bring a medium pot of water to a boil over high heat. Add the walnuts and blanch them for 3 minutes. Drain the walnuts in a colander.
2. In a wok, combine the sugar, salt, and ⅓ cup of water and heat the mixture over medium heat, stirring with a spatula to dissolve the sugar. Add the walnuts to the wok, flipping them so they're coated in the syrup. Simmer the walnuts for 5 to 7 minutes, uncovered, until all of the water evaporates.
3. With the walnuts still in the wok, add the oil, heat it over medium heat, and fry the walnuts for about 5 minutes, or until their color darkens. As the walnuts fry, flip them constantly to separate them into individual pieces.
4. Using a spider strainer or slotted spoon, transfer the walnuts to a plate. Sprinkle the sesame seeds on top. The walnuts will become crunchy once cooled.
5. Store the walnuts in a sealed glass jar in the pantry for up to 1 week.

Chapter 4
Egg and Tofu

Salt and Black Pepper Tofu

Prep time: 5 minutes | Cook time: 15 minutes | Serves 6

- Tofu Brine
- 14 ounces firm tofu, sliced
- ¼ teaspoon garlic powder
- ½ teaspoon onion powder
- ½ teaspoon salt
- 1 teaspoon sugar
- 1¼ cups warm water
- ½ teaspoon sesame oil
- 1 teaspoon Shaoxing wine

TOFU SEASONING

- ¾ teaspoon salt
- ¾ teaspoon ground white pepper
- ¼ teaspoon ground Sichuan peppercorn
- ¼ teaspoon sand ginger powder
- 2 tablespoons all-purpose flour
- 2 tablespoons cornstarch

FOR THE DISH

- 4 tablespoons vegetable oil
- 5 garlic cloves, chopped
- 1 long hot green pepper, sliced
- 1 shallot, sliced
- 1 scallion, chopped
- 1 tablespoon cilantro, chopped

1. Mix tofu with all of its brine Prep time: 5 minutes | Cook time: 5 minutes | Serves 4 in a bowl and cover to marinate for 2 hours.
2. Whisk flour with cornstarch, peppercorn, white pepper, salt, and ginger powder in a bowl.
3. To cook the tofu, heat oil in a Cantonese wok.
4. Dredge the marinated tofu through the flour mixture and sear in the wok until golden from both sides.
5. Stir in rest of the Prep time: 5 minutes | Cook time: 5 minutes | Serves 4 and cook for 5 minutes.
6. Serve warm.

Tofu Avocado Salad

Prep time: 5 minutes | Cook time: 5 minutes | Serves 4

- 7 ounces silken tofu, sliced
- 1 ripe avocado, peeled and sliced
- 2 garlic cloves, grated
- 1 teaspoon ginger, grated
- 2 tablespoons light soy sauce
- 1 teaspoon sesame oil
- ½ teaspoon sugar
- ½ teaspoon Chinese black vinegar
- ¼ teaspoon white pepper
- 2 teaspoons water
- Salt, to taste
- 1 scallion, finely chopped

1. Sauté tofu with sesame oil in a Mandarin wok for 5 minutes.
2. Toss tofu with rest of the salad Prep time: 5 minutes | Cook time: 5 minutes | Serves 4 in a salad bowl.
3. Mix well and serve.
4. Enjoy.

Gingered Tofu

Prep time: 5 minutes | Cook time: 25 minutes| Serves 6

- 21 ounces firm tofu, cut into cubes
- 2 tablespoons oil
- 4 ginger slices
- 1 tablespoon Shaoxing wine
- 2 tablespoons Chinese black vinegar
- 3 tablespoons light soy sauce
- 4 tablespoons sugar
- 5 tablespoons water

1. Sauté ginger with oil in a Cantonese wok for 30 seconds.
2. Stir in tofu, and sauté for 10 minutes until it turns golden.
3. Add wine, black vinegar, soy sauce, water, and sugar.
4. Cover and cook for 15 minutes over medium low heat.
5. Serve warm.

Chinese Tomato Egg Stir-Fry

Prep time: 5 minutes | Cook time: 8 minutes| Serves 4

- 4 tomatoes, diced
- 1 scallion, chopped
- 4 eggs
- ¾ teaspoons salt
- ¼ teaspoon white pepper
- ½ teaspoon sesame oil
- 1 teaspoon Shaoxing wine
- 3 tablespoons vegetable oil
- 2 teaspoons sugar
- ¼–½ cup water

1. Sauté tomatoes and scallions with oil in a Cantonese wok for 2 minutes.
2. Beat eggs with salt, white pepper, sesame oil, wine, sugar, and water in a bowl.
3. Pour the eggs mixture into the wok and stir cook for 5 minutes.
4. Serve warm.

Kung Pao Tofu

Prep time: 5 minutes | Cook time: 15 minutes| Serves 6

TOFU

- 14 ounces firm tofu
- 1/3 cup cornstarch
- ¼ teaspoon garlic powder
- ¼ teaspoon onion powder
- 1/8 teaspoon five-spice powder
- ¼ teaspoon salt
- ¼ cup water

FOR THE REST

- 1 tablespoon soy sauce
- ½ teaspoon dark soy sauce
- 2 teaspoons sugar
- ¼ teaspoon salt
- 1½ teaspoon rice vinegar
- ½ teaspoon sesame oil
- 2 teaspoons cornstarch
- 2/3 cup warm water
- ¼ cup peanut oil
- 1 cup blanched peanuts
- 2 medium carrots chopped
- 1 tablespoon ginger, minced
- 3–5 dried chili peppers, chopped
- 3 garlic cloves, chopped
- 3 scallions, diced
- 1 teaspoon Sichuan peppercorn powder

1. For tofu, mix cornstarch with water, salt, five-spice powder, onion powder, and garlic powder in a bowl.
2. Mix soy sauces, sugar, salt, rice vinegar, cornstarch, sesame oil, and warm water in a bowl.
3. Sauté peanut with ¼ cup peanut oil in a Cantonese wok for 5 minutes, then transfer to a plate.
4. Sear the tofu in the same oil until golden-brown, then transfer to a plate.
5. Now sauté ginger and chili peppers with 1½ tablespoons peanut oil in a Cantonese wok for 1 minute.
6. Add tofu, peanuts, and prepared sauce.
7. Mix well and garnish with peppercorn.
8. Enjoy.

Braised Tofu

Prep time: 15 minutes | Cook time: 8 minutes| Serves 6

- 1 pound silken tofu
- 2 cups oil, for frying
- 1 cup chicken stock
- 1 tablespoon oyster sauce
- 1½ tablespoon soy sauce
- 1 teaspoon dark soy sauce
- ½ teaspoon sesame oil
- ¼ teaspoon sugar
- ¼ teaspoon salt
- 3 small ginger slices, 1/8 inch thick
- 3 garlic cloves, finely minced
- 2 scallions, chopped
- 4 fresh shiitake mushrooms
- 1 medium carrot, thinly sliced
- 2/3 cup fresh winter bamboo shoots
- 1 tablespoon Shaoxing wine
- ½ cup snap peas
- 1½ tablespoon cornstarch

1. In a deep pan, heat 2 cups oil and deep fry the tofu until golden-brown.
2. Transfer the tofu to a plate and set it aside.
3. Sauté ginger with oil in a Cantonese wok for 15 seconds.
4. Stir in mushrooms, carrots, scallions, and bamboo shoots, and cook for 30 seconds.
5. Add snap peas, wine, all the sauces, sesame oil, sugar, and salt, then cook for 4 minutes
6. Mix cornstarch with water in a bowl and pour into the wok.
7. Stir and cook for 1–2 minutes until the mixture thickens.
8. Toss in deep fried tofu and mix well to coat.
9. Serve warm.

Tofu with Black Bean Sauce

Prep time: 5 minutes | Cook time: 15 minutes | Serves 4

- 1 pound firm tofu, diced
- 3 tablespoons oil
- 2 garlic cloves, minced
- 2 tablespoons fermented black beans, rinsed
- 2 scallions, whites and greens separated
- 3 dried red chilies, deseeded and chopped
- 1 tablespoon Shaoxing wine
- ½ tablespoon light soy sauce
- ½ teaspoon sesame oil
- ¼ teaspoon ground white pepper
- ¼ teaspoon sugar
- 1 teaspoon cornstarch, mixed with 2 tablespoons water

1. Sauté garlic with oil in a large wok for 30 seconds.
2. Stir in tofu and cook it for 5 minutes until golden-brown.
3. Add black beans, wine, soy sauce, red chillies, white pepper, sugar, and cover to a cook for 3 minutes.
4. Stir in cornstarch, mix well, and cook for 2 minutes.
5. Garnish with scallions.
6. Serve warm.

Chinese Tofu Salad

Prep time: 5 minutes | Cook time: 15 minutes | Serves 4

- 1 cup red bell pepper, julienned
- 1 cup red onion, sliced
- 1 cup carrot, julienned
- 1 cup cucumber, julienned
- 1 cup celery, julienned
- 8 ounces spiced tofu, shredded
- 1 tablespoon light olive oil
- 1 teaspoon garlic, minced
- 1 ½ teaspoons sugar
- ¼ teaspoon ground white pepper
- 2 tablespoons light soy sauce
- 1 tablespoon Chinese black vinegar
- 1 teaspoon sesame oil
- 1 tablespoon toasted sesame seeds
- ¼ cup cilantro, chopped

1. Sauté garlic, celery, carrot, onion, and bell pepper with oil in a Cantonese wok for 5 minutes.
2. Stir in tofu and sauté for 5 minutes.
3. Add soy sauce, white pepper, sugar, black vinegar, and cook for 5 minutes.
4. Remove it with from the heat and toss in cucumber.
5. Garnish with sesame seeds and cilantro.
6. Serve warm.

Chinese Chives Eggs Stir-Fry

Prep time: 5 minutes | Cook time: 10 minutes| Serves 6

- 5 large eggs
- 1/8 teaspoon sugar
- ½ teaspoon salt
- 1 teaspoon Shaoxing wine
- ¼ teaspoon ground white pepper
- ¼ teaspoon sesame oil
- 4 teaspoons water
- 2 cups Chinese chives, chopped
- 4 tablespoons vegetable oil

1. Beat eggs with sugar, salt, wine, white pepper, water, chives, and sesame oil in a bowl.
2. Set up a wok on medium heat and add vegetable oil to heat.
3. Pour the egg-wine mixture and stir-fry for 5–7 minutes until eggs are set.
4. Serve warm.

Silken Tofu Salad

Prep time: 10 minutes| Cook time: 5 minutes| Serves 6

- 1 (16oz / 454g) block silken tofu or ⅔ recipe Tofu from Scratch
- 3 tablespoons chopped preserved mustard stem (zha cai)
- 2 tablespoons sliced scallions
- 2 tablespoons chopped fresh cilantro
- 2 tablespoons Chinese light soy sauce
- 1 tablespoon sesame oil
- 2 teaspoons black vinegar

1. Drain the tofu and place it upside down on a deep plate.
2. Cut the tofu in half lengthwise, then cut it crosswise into ½-inch-thick slices, but leave the slices in the shape of the original block of tofu.
3. Sprinkle the chopped preserved mustard stem, scallion, and cilantro on top of the tofu.
4. In a small bowl, mix the soy sauce, sesame oil, and vinegar together.
5. Pour the dressing over the tofu. Serve immediately.

Shui Zheng Dan (Water-Steamed Egg)

Prep time: 5 minutes | Cook time: 20 minutes| Serves 3

- 1 cup water
- 2 large eggs
- 1 cup chicken broth or water
- 1 scallion, white and green parts, thinly sliced (optional)
- 1 teaspoon oyster sauce or light soy sauce
- 1 teaspoon sesame oil

1. Pour the water into the Instant Pot and place a trivet inside.
2. In a 4-cup pressure-safe bowl, lightly beat the eggs. Gently stir in the broth to avoid adding air bubbles into the egg. If you don't like raw scallion as a garnish, add the chopped scallion (if using) to the egg mixture.
3. Wrap the bowl with aluminum foil and lower the bowl onto the trivet.
4. Lock the lid. Program to pressure cook for 10 minutes on high pressure.
5. When the timer sounds, quick release the pressure. Carefully remove the lid and take the steamed eggs out of the pot.
6. Drizzle with oyster sauce and sesame oil and sprinkle with the raw scallion (if using, and you did not already add it).

Stir-Fried Tomato and Eggs

Prep time: 5 minutes | Cook time: 5 minutes| Serves: 4

- 4 eggs
- Pinch salt
- Pinch pepper
- 1 teaspoon Shaoxing wine
- 2 tablespoons peanut oil
- 2 medium tomatoes, cut into wedges
- ½ teaspoon sugar
- 1 scallion, cut into 1-inch pieces

1. In a medium bowl, add the eggs and the Shaoxing wine. Season them with the salt and pepper and beat together until well combined.
2. In a wok over medium-high heat, heat the peanut oil.
3. Pour the egg mixture into the wok and allow the bottom to cook before gently scrambling.
4. Just before the egg starts to cook all the way through, remove it from the wok.
5. Toss the tomato wedges into the wok and stir-fry until they become a little soft.
6. Return the scrambled eggs to the wok with the tomato, then sprinkle the sugar over the stir-fry.
7. Turn off the heat, add the scallion, and give one last stir before transferring to a serving plate.

Five-Spice Soy Tea Eggs

Prep time: 10 minutes, plus 30 minutes to soak | Cook time: 50 minutes| Makes 6 eggs

- 2 cups water
- ¼ cup light soy sauce
- 2 tablespoons sugar
- 1 tablespoon rice wine
- 2 teaspoons oolong tea, or 2 black tea bags
- 1 teaspoon Chinese five-spice powder
- 1 (1-inch) piece fresh ginger, thinly sliced
- ½ teaspoon salt
- 6 large eggs

1. In the Instant Pot, combine the water, soy sauce, sugar, wine, tea, five-spice powder, ginger, and salt. Place a steamer basket or a trivet inside and arrange the eggs in it.
2. Lock the lid. Program to Steam or Egg for 5 minutes on high pressure. While the eggs cook, prepare an ice bath.
3. When the timer sounds, quick release the pressure and carefully remove the lid. Using a slotted spoon, transfer the eggs to the ice bath.
4. Gently tap the eggs on a hard surface to create small cracks in the shells, but not so hard that the eggshells fall apart.
5. Transfer the brine to a heatproof container, add the eggs, and let soak for at least 30 minutes before serving.
6. Refrigerate any leftover eggs in the brine overnight, covered, and discard the brine the next day.

Ma Po Tofu

Prep time: 10 minutes | Cook time: 15 minutes| Serves: 4

FOR THE SAUCE
- 1 teaspoon black bean paste
- 1 teaspoon spicy bean paste
- 1 teaspoon soy sauce
- 1 teaspoon oyster sauce
- Pinch ground black pepper
- 2 teaspoons cornstarch
- ¼ cup water
- ½ teaspoon sugar

FOR THE STIR-FRY
- 1 tablespoon peanut oil
- 2 garlic cloves, minced
- ½ pound ground pork
- 1 package firm tofu, cut into 1- to 1½-inch cubes
- 1 scallion, chopped

1. In a small bowl, prepare the sauce by mixing together the black bean paste, spicy bean paste, soy sauce, oyster sauce, black pepper, cornstarch, water, and sugar. Set it aside.
2. In a wok over medium-high heat, heat the peanut oil.
3. Stir-fry the garlic and ground pork until the pork is fully cooked.
4. Add the sauce and stir well.
5. When the sauce starts to thicken, add the tofu. Give it a gentle quick stir, taking care not to break the tofu.
6. Remove from the heat and transfer to a serving plate.
7. Garnish with the chopped scallion.

Chapter 5
Poultry

Three-Color Shredded Chicken (San Si Ji Diang)

Prep time: 15 minutes | Cook time: 5 minutes | Serves 4

- For the marinade
- 2 boneless, skinless chicken breasts
- 1 large egg white, beaten
- 1 tablespoon potato starch
- 1 tablespoon water
- 1 teaspoon Shaoxing cooking wine or dry sherry
- 1 teaspoon sea salt
- For the stir-fry
- 2 tablespoons cooking oil
- 1 scallion, both white and green parts, finely chopped
- 1 (1-inch) piece peeled fresh ginger, minced
- 2 garlic cloves, minced
- 1 cup julienned green bell pepper
- 1 cup julienned carrot
- 1 tablespoon Shaoxing cooking wine or dry sherry
- 1 teaspoon sugar
- 1 teaspoon sea salt
- ½ teaspoon ground white pepper

TO MAKE THE MARINADE

1. Firm up the chicken by putting it in the freezer for 15 minutes to make it easier to slice. Then, cut the chicken into slices and cut each slice into ¼-inch-thick strips.
2. In a medium bowl, combine the egg white, potato starch, 1 tablespoon of water, wine, and salt. Add the chicken and toss to coat. Let the chicken marinate while preparing the other ingredients.

TO MAKE THE STIR-FRY

1. In the wok, heat the oil over high heat until it shimmers. Add the chicken pieces and stir-fry until they separate from each other, about 1 minute.
2. Add the scallion, ginger, and garlic, and stir-fry for 1 minute. Add the bell pepper and carrot. Add the wine, sugar, salt, and white pepper. Stir-fry for 2 minutes.
3. Transfer the chicken to a serving plate and serve hot.

Five-Spice Orange Duck Meatballs

Prep time: 15 minutes | Cook time: 5 minutes | Serves 4

- 1 pound ground duck
- 2 tablespoons Shaoxing cooking wine
- Zest and juice from 1 orange
- 1 tablespoon chopped fresh ginger
- 3 garlic cloves, crushed and chopped
- 1 tablespoon soy sauce
- 1 tablespoon Chinese five-spice powder
- 1 teaspoon spicy sesame oil
- ½ cup panko bread crumbs, divided
- Oil, for deep-frying
- 2 tablespoons orange marmalade
- 2 tablespoons hoisin sauce
- ¼ cup ketchup

1. In a medium bowl, combine the duck, wine, orange zest and juice, ginger, garlic, soy sauce, five-spice powder, sesame oil, and ¼ cup panko bread crumbs. Mix well with chopsticks (but do not mash the mixture).
2. Form 12 to 16 (1½-inch diameter) meatballs. Roll each in the remaining ¼ cup of panko bread crumbs to coat.
3. In the wok, heat 1 inch of oil over high heat until the tip of a wooden chopstick dipped into the oil creates bubbles. Fry the meatballs for 3 minutes. Turn them and fry for another 2 or 3 minutes, until golden brown, adding oil as needed to cover the meatballs halfway.
4. In a small bowl, combine the marmalade, hoisin sauce, and ketchup for a glaze or dip to serve with the meatballs.

Crispy Chicken and Red Chiles

Prep time: 20 minutes | Cook time: 20 minutes | Serves 4

FOR THE CHICKEN

- 2 pounds chicken, cut into 1-inch pieces
- 3 tablespoons Shaoxing cooking wine or dry sherry
- 3 tablespoons dark soy sauce
- 1 cup potato starch
- 1 tablespoon freshly ground Sichuan peppercorns
- 1 tablespoon ground red chili powder or cayenne pepper
- 2 teaspoons sea salt
- Cooking oil, for deep-frying
- For the sauce
- 10 garlic cloves, sliced
- 1 teaspoon freshly ground Sichuan peppercorns
- 3 tablespoons doubanjiang (Chinese chili bean paste)
- 2 tablespoons minced fresh ginger
- 1 cup dried red chiles
- ¼ teaspoon sea salt

TO MAKE THE CHICKEN

1. In a large bowl, combine the chicken, wine, and soy sauce, toss to coat, and let sit to marinate while you prepare the rest of the dish.
2. In a small, shallow bowl, combine the potato starch, ground Sichuan peppercorns, chili powder, and salt.
3. Remove the chicken from the marinade a few pieces at a time (shaking off excess marinade), dredge in the spiced starch mixture, and put on a plate.
4. In the wok, heat 2 inches of oil over high heat until it shimmers. Fry the chicken, turning occasionally, for about 10 minutes, until golden.
5. Deep-fry the chicken in two to three batches, allowing enough room for the chicken to cook on all sides. Once cooked, transfer the chicken to a paper towel–lined plate. Once all the chicken is fried, transfer the remaining oil to a heatproof jar or bowl. Return 3 tablespoons of oil to the wok.

TO MAKE THE SAUCE

6. In the wok, heat the oil on high heat until it shimmers.
7. Add the garlic and stir-fry until fragrant, about 10 seconds. Add the ground Sichuan peppercorns, doubanjiang, and ginger, and stir-fry until the sauce becomes a red-orange color.
8. Return the chicken pieces to the wok and toss to coat with the sauce. Add the dried red chiles and salt, and stir-fry for 2 minutes. Serve hot.

Cashew Chicken

Prep time: 10 minutes | Cook time: 10 minutes | Serves 2 to 4

- 2 tablespoons vegetable oil
- 3 garlic cloves, crushed and chopped
- 1 tablespoon crushed and chopped fresh ginger
- 1 medium carrot, roll-cut into ½-inch pieces
- 1 pound boneless chicken thighs, cut into 1-inch cubes
- 1 medium onion, halved and cut into ½-inch slices
- 1 red bell pepper, diced into ½-inch pieces
- 1 cup dry-roasted cashews
- 1 cup chopped bok choy (about ½-inch pieces)
- 4 tablespoons soy sauce
- 2 tablespoons honey
- 1 tablespoon toasted sesame oil
- 1 teaspoon cornstarch
- 1 bunch (6 to 8) scallions, cut into ½-inch pieces
- Steamed rice, for serving

1. In the wok, heat the vegetable oil over high heat until it shimmers.
2. Add the garlic, ginger, and carrot and stir-fry for 1 minute. Add the chicken and onion and stir-fry for 1 minute. Add the bell pepper and cashews and stir-fry for 1 minute. Add the bok choy and stir-fry for 1 minute.
3. In a medium bowl, whisk together the soy sauce, honey, sesame oil, and cornstarch. Add the sauce to the wok and stir for about 2 minutes, until a glaze forms.
4. Remove from the heat and stir in the scallions.
5. Serve over steamed rice.

Sweet-And-Sour Chicken (Gu Lao Ji)

Prep time: 10 minutes | Cook time: 5 minutes | Serves 4

- 1 pound boneless, skinless chicken thighs, cut into ¼-inch pieces across the grain
- 2 tablespoons brown sugar
- 2 tablespoons Shaoxing cooking wine
- 2 tablespoons rice vinegar
- 1 tablespoon light soy sauce
- ¼ cup ketchup
- 2 tablespoons cooking oil
- 1 tablespoon chopped, fresh ginger
- 2 garlic cloves, crushed and chopped
- 1 medium onion, cut into ½-inch pieces
- 1 medium red bell pepper, cut into ½-inch pieces
- 1 teaspoon cornstarch
- 4 scallions, both white and green parts, cut into ¼-inch pieces
- Rice or noodles, for serving

1. In a bowl, combine the sliced chicken, brown sugar, wine, vinegar, soy sauce, and ketchup.
2. In the wok, heat the oil over medium-high heat until it shimmers. Add the ginger, garlic, and chicken, reserving any liquid, and stir-fry for 2 minutes, until fragrant.
3. Add the onion and stir-fry for 1 minute. Add the bell pepper and stir-fry for 1 minute, until the onion pieces begin to separate.
4. Add the cornstarch and reserved liquid to the wok and stir-fry for about 2 minutes, until a glaze is formed, and the chicken is cooked through.
5. Add the scallions and serve over rice or noodles.

Chinese Celery, Mushrooms & Fish Stir Fry

Prep time: 5 minutes | Cook time: 5 minutes| Serves 2

- 1/2 pound fish fillets
  1 cup Chinese celery
- 1 cup mushrooms sliced in half
- 1/2 cup peppers sliced diagonally
- 1 tsp. oil

1. Marinade fish in a Superfoods marinade. Stir fry drained fish in coconut oil for few minutes, add all vegetables and stir fry for 2 more minutes.
2. Add the rest of the marinade and stir fry for a minute. Serve with brown rice or quinoa.

Crispy Steamed Duck

Prep time: 10 minutes | Cook time: 20 minutes | Serves 2 to 4

- 4 boneless, skin-on duck breasts
- 2 tablespoons cornstarch
- 1 tablespoon Chinese five-spice powder
- 5 scallions, both white and green parts, sliced
- Steamed rice, noodles, or pancakes, for serving
- Hoisin sauce, for dipping

1. Score the duck skin with shallow crosscuts about ¼ inch apart.
2. Place the wok or a pot fitted with a steamer basket over high heat. Add water until it is 1 inch below the bottom of the basket.
3. When the water boils, immediately place the duck, skin-side down, in the basket, cover, and steam for 10 minutes, or until the water is almost gone. Remove the duck and steamer basket, but leave the remaining liquid.
4. Reduce the heat to medium for about 3 minutes more to evaporate the remaining water, leaving just the duck fat.
5. Transfer the duck to a large zip-top bag with the cornstarch and five-spice powder. Massage for 2 minutes.
6. Heat the duck fat over medium-high heat until it shimmers. Add the coated duck, skin-side up, and fry for 1 minute. Flip the duck over and fry for 2 minutes, or until the skin is crispy brown.
7. Thinly slice the duck or cut it into cubes, sprinkle it with scallions, and serve with steamed rice, noodles, or pancakes, and hoisin sauce for dipping.

Chicken, Zucchini, Carrots and Baby Corn Stir Fry

Prep time: 5 minutes | Cook time: 5 minutes| Serves 2

- 1/2 pound chicken
  1 cup zucchini
- 1/2 cup sliced carrots
- 1/2 cup baby corn
- 1 tbsp. chopped cilantro
- 1 tsp. oil

1. Marinade chicken in a Superfoods marinade. Stir fry drained chicken in coconut oil for few minutes, add all vegetables and stir fry for 2 more minutes.
2. Add the rest of the marinade and stir fry for a minute. Serve with brown rice or quinoa over bed of lettuce.

Green Tea Smoked Lemon Chicken

Prep time: 10 minutes | Cook time: 15 minutes | Serves 4

- ¼ cup uncooked long-grain white rice
- ¼ cup green tea leaves
- 2 tablespoons all-purpose flour
- 2 tablespoons brown sugar
- Coarsely chopped zest and juice of 1 lemon
- 1 pound boneless, skinless chicken thighs (3 or 4 thighs)
- 2 tablespoons light soy sauce
- 2 tablespoons Shaoxing cooking wine
- 1 tablespoon cornstarch
- 2 tablespoons cooking oil
- 1 tablespoon chopped, fresh ginger
- 2 garlic cloves, crushed and chopped
- 4 scallions, both white and green parts, cut into ¼-inch pieces
- Rice or noodles, for serving

1. Combine the rice, tea leaves, flour, brown sugar, and lemon zest on a square piece of aluminum foil and roll the edges up to form the foil into a shallow, ½-inch-deep saucer. The top should be open. Place the foil saucer in the bottom of the wok.
2. Place a rack inside the wok and place the chicken thighs on a rack above the mixture. Cover with a domed lid.
3. If you're cooking indoors, open windows near the stove and turn your exhaust fan on high. If you don't have a way to exhaust air outside, you will want to do the next steps outdoors.
4. Turn the heat on high until the mixture smokes. First the smoke will be white, then light yellow, then darker yellow. When it turns dark yellow (about 5 minutes), turn the heat on low and start timing.
5. For a light smoke, set a timer for 3 minutes. For a heavier smoke, add 5 to 10 minutes more. Turn the heat off and let rest for 1 minute.
6. Remove the chicken and slice it into ¼-inch pieces across the grain.
7. In a medium bowl, combine the sliced, smoked chicken, lemon juice, soy sauce, wine, and cornstarch.
8. In the wok, heat the oil over medium-high heat until it shimmers. Add the ginger, garlic, and chicken, reserving any liquid. Stir-fry for 2 minutes, until the chicken is lightly browned and fragrant.
9. Add the reserved liquid and stir-fry for 1 minute, until the chicken is cooked through and a glaze forms.
10. Add the scallions and stir-fry for 1 minute to mix. Serve over rice or noodles.

Tangerine Peel Chicken

Prep time: 5 minutes | Cook time: 25 minutes | Serves 4

4 tangerines or 2 oranges (preferably organic) with peels, cut into quarters
1 tablespoon peeled and chopped fresh ginger
5 garlic cloves, peeled
¾ cup coconut sugar
¾ cup chicken broth
½ cup plum sauce, hoisin sauce, or Korean BBQ sauce
1½ teaspoons sriracha
1 teaspoon raw apple cider vinegar
¼ teaspoon five-spice powder
2 tablespoons extra-virgin olive oil
8 boneless, skinless chicken thighs
Sea salt
Ground black pepper

1. Preheat your broiler.
2. Combine the tangerines, ginger, garlic, sugar, broth, plum sauce, sriracha, vinegar, and five-spice powder in a blender. Blend until the mixture is really smooth. Set aside.
3. Heat the oil in a large sauté pan over medium-high heat.
4. Season the chicken generously with salt and pepper. Add the chicken to the pan. Cook until it is brown on one side, about 5 minutes. Flip and brown the other side, about 5 minutes more.
5. When the chicken is browned, pour enough of the tangerine sauce into the pan so that the chicken is mostly covered. Stir to coat the chicken.
6. Cover the pan and cook until the chicken is cooked through, about 15 minutes.
7. Using tongs, remove the chicken from the pan, shaking off any excess sauce, and transfer it to a rimmed baking sheet.
8. Broil until the chicken just starts to char, about 3 minutes. Serve and enjoy!

Wok-Fried Duck Breasts and Hoisin Sauce with Bok Choy

Prep time: 10 minutes | Cook time: 15 minutes | Serves 4

- 4 (4-ounce) boneless, skin-on duck breasts
- 2 tablespoons soy sauce
- 2 tablespoons Shaoxing cooking wine
- 1 tablespoon toasted sesame oil
- 1 teaspoon cornstarch
- 1 tablespoon chopped, fresh ginger
- 3 garlic cloves, crushed and chopped
- 1 medium red onion, cut into ½-inch pieces
- 2 cups bok choy, sliced into ½-inch pieces
- 2 tablespoons hoisin sauce
- 4 scallions, both white and green parts, sliced into ¼-inch pieces
- Rice or noodles, for serving

1. Lightly score the skin of the duck breasts with perpendicular cuts ¼ inch apart.
2. In a large bowl or zip-top bag, combine the soy sauce, wine, sesame oil, cornstarch, and scored duck breasts and mix well. (Massaging them in a plastic bag works really well.)
3. Transfer the duck breasts to the wok on medium-high heat, skin-side down, and cook until you hear the juices begin to sizzle, about 2 minutes. Once sizzling, let the breasts cook for another 3 minutes, until the skin is light brown.
4. Turn the breasts over and let them cook for 1 additional minute, then remove them from the wok and slice into ¼-inch pieces across the grain.
5. Drain all but 2 tablespoons of fat from the wok and turn the heat on high.
6. Add the ginger, garlic, and onion and stir-fry for 1 minute, until fragrant.
7. Add the bok choy and stir-fry for 1 minute.
8. Return the sliced duck to the wok and stir-fry for 1 minute, until well mixed.
9. Add the hoisin sauce and scallions and stir-fry for 1 minute, until well mixed. Serve over rice or noodles.

Tea-Smoked Duck Breast (Zhangcha Ya)

Prep time: 10 minutes | Cook time: 15 minutes | Serves 4

- 4 boneless, skin-on duck breasts
- 1 teaspoon fine sea salt
- 2 tablespoons loose jasmine tea
- ¼ cup uncooked long-grain white rice
- ¼ cup brown sugar
- 2 tablespoons all-purpose flour
- Plum sauce, for dipping

1. Lightly score the duck skin with perpendicular cuts ¼-inch apart, making sure not to cut down into the meat.
2. Place the breasts skin-side down in the wok and heat on medium-high until the fat begins to render and sizzle. Then reduce the heat to medium and cook for 5 minutes.
3. Drain the fat from the wok. Turn the duck breast over and cook for another 5 minutes.
4. Remove the duck breasts, drain the fat, and wipe out the wok.
5. Combine the tea leaves, rice, brown sugar, and flour on a square piece of aluminum foil and roll the edges up to form the foil into a shallow, ½-inch-deep saucer. The top should be open. Place the foil saucer in the bottom of the wok.
6. Place a rack inside the wok and put the duck breasts on the rack. Cover the wok with a domed lid.
7. If you're cooking indoors, open any windows near the stove and turn your exhaust fan on high. If you don't have a way to exhaust air outside, do the next steps outdoors.
8. Turn the heat on high. As the mixture heats, it will begin to smoke. At first, the smoke will be white, then light yellow, then darker yellow. When it turns dark yellow (after about 5 minutes), turn the heat to low.
9. For a light smoke, set a timer for 3 minutes. For heavier smoke, smoke the breasts for 5 to 10 minutes longer.
10. Remove and slice the breasts into ½-inch pieces across the grain and serve with plum sauce.

Simple Roast Chicken and Kale
Prep time: 5 minutes | Cook time: 45 minutes | Serves 4

- 1 very large head or 2 small heads lacinato (black) kale (about 1½ pounds total), tough center ribs removed and discarded, leaves cut into large pieces
- 4 bone-in, skin-on, chicken leg quarters or 8 chicken thighs
- 2 tablespoons extra-virgin olive oil
- Sea salt
- Ground black pepper
- 6 medium red potatoes, scrubbed and quartered
- 10 garlic cloves, peeled and smashed
- ¼ cup fresh lemon juice
- 2 large lemons, thinly sliced
- 8 thyme sprigs

1. Preheat the oven to 425°F.
2. Spread out the kale in the bottom of a 9-by-13-inch baking dish (it's okay if it's really full, because the kale will shrink up a lot).
3. Brush the chicken with the olive oil and season generously with salt and pepper.
4. Arrange the chicken pieces on top of the kale so that they do not touch.
5. Put the potatoes and garlic in a medium bowl. Add the lemon juice, season with salt and pepper to taste, and stir to combine.
6. Arrange the potatoes and garlic around the chicken pieces, on top of the kale.
7. Lay the lemon slices on top of the chicken pieces. Place the thyme sprigs on top of the chicken and potatoes.
8. Roast until the chicken is crispy and an instant-read thermometer inserted into the thickest part registers 170°F, about 45 minutes.
9. Transfer to a platter and enjoy!

Chicken Edamame Stir Fry
Prep time: 5 minutes | Cook time: 10 minutes | Serves 2

- 1/2 pound chicken
  1 cup edamame pre-cooked in boiling water for 3 minutes
- 1/2 cup sliced carrots
- 1 tsp. oil

1. Marinade chicken in a Superfoods marinade. Stir fry drained chicken in coconut oil for few minutes, add all vegetables and stir fry for 2 more minutes.
2. Add the rest of the marinade and stir fry for a minute. Serve with brown rice or quinoa.

Garlic Chicken (Suan Ji)
Prep time: 10 minutes | Cook time: 5 minutes | Serves 4

- 1 pound boneless, skinless chicken thighs, cut into ¼-inch pieces across the grain
- 2 tablespoons dark soy sauce
- 2 tablespoons cooking oil
- 1 tablespoon chopped, fresh ginger
- 4 garlic cloves, crushed and chopped
- 4 scallions, both white and green parts, cut into ¼-inch pieces
- Rice or noodles, for serving

1. In a medium bowl, combine the chicken and dark soy sauce.
2. In the wok, heat the oil over medium-high heat until it shimmers.
3. Add the ginger, garlic, and chicken and stir-fry for 3 minutes, until browned and fragrant.
4. Add the scallions and stir-fry for 1 minute to mix. Serve over rice or noodles.

Chicken, Mushrooms & Asparagus Stir Fry
Prep time: 5 minutes | Cook time: 5 minutes | Serves 2

- 1/2 pound chicken breast meat
  1 cups sliced Asparagus
- 1/2 cup sliced carrot
- 1/2 cup sliced mushrooms
- 1 Tbsp. coconut oil

1. Marinade chicken in a Superfoods marinade. Stir fry drained chicken in coconut oil for few minutes, add all vegetables and stir fry for 2 more minutes.
2. Add the rest of the marinade and stir fry for a minute. Serve with brown rice or quinoa.

Chicken, Green Beans & Snow Peas Stir Fry
Prep time: 5 minutes | Cook time: 5 minutes | Serves 2

- 1/2 pound chicken
  1 cup halved asparagus
- 1 cup snow peas
- 1 tbsp. sliced green onions
- 1 tbsp. coconut oil

1. Marinade chicken in a Superfoods marinade. Stir fry drained chicken and asparagus in coconut oil for few minutes, add snow peas and stir fry for 4-5 more minutes.
2. Add the rest of the marinade and stir fry for a minute. Sprinkle with green onions. Serve with brown rice or quinoa.

Chinese Fried Ribs

Prep time: 5 minutes | Cook time: 10 minutes| Serves 4

- 2 pounds pork ribs, cut into 1-inch nuggets
- 1 large piece red fermented bean curd
- ½ teaspoon ground white pepper
- 1 teaspoon sesame oil
- 1 teaspoon five spice powder
- 2 tablespoons Shaoxing wine
- 1 tablespoon soy sauce
- 1 tablespoon maple syrup
- ½ teaspoon garlic powder
- ½ teaspoon onion powder
- ½ teaspoon baking soda
- ¼ cup cornstarch
- 3 cups canola oil

1. Mix bean curd, white pepper, sesame oil, spice powder, wine, soy sauce, maple syrup, garlic powder, onion powder, baking soda, and cornstarch in a bowl.
2. Stir in pork ribs and mix well to coat.
3. Cover the pork and marinate for 1 hour in the refrigerator.
4. Add 3 cups canola oil in a deep wok and heat up to 350°F.
5. Deep fry the pork chunks for 7 minutes until golden-brown.
6. Serve warm.

Cantonese Pork Knuckles

Prep time: 10 minutes | Cook time: 1 hour, 33 minutes | Serves 4

- 1 pound ginger
- 5 cups Chinese sweet vinegar
- ½ cup Chinese black vinegar
- 2 pounds pork knuckle
- 2 tablespoons Shaoxing wine
- 6 hard-boiled eggs
- Salt, to taste

1. Boil ginger with sweet vinegar and black vinegar in a Cantonese wok for 90 minutes on a simmer.
2. Add pork knuckles, wine, and enough water to cover the pork, and cook for 3 minutes.
3. Cover and cook for another 90 minutes over medium heat.
4. Add the hard-boiled eggs to the pork and cook the mixture to a boil.
5. Serve warm.

Beijing Lamb Skewers

Prep time: 5 minutes | Cook time: 15 minutes| Serves 4

- 1 pound lamb shoulder, diced
- 2 teaspoons cumin seeds
- 1 tablespoon dried chili flakes
- Salt, to taste
- 1 tablespoon oil
- Bamboo skewers

1. Grind cumin seeds with chili flakes, oil, and salt in a mortar with pestle.
2. Rub this mixture over the lamb cubes and cover to a marinate for 30 minutes.
3. Thread the lamb cubes on the skewers.
4. Sear the lamb skewers for 6 minutes in a preheated and greased wok.
5. Enjoy.

Xinjiang Cumin Lamb

Prep time: 5 minutes | Cook time: 25 minutes| Serves 4

- Marinate the Lamb
- 1 pound lamb shoulder, cut into 2-inch pieces
- 1 tablespoon cumin
- 1½ teaspoon cornstarch
- 1 tablespoon oil
- 1 tablespoon light soy sauce
- 1 tablespoon Shaoxing rice wine

- For the Dish
- 2 tablespoons cumin seeds
- 2 tablespoons oil
- 2 red chili peppers, chopped
- ½ teaspoon Sichuan red pepper flakes
- ¼ teaspoon sugar
- 2 scallions, chopped
- Large handful of chopped cilantros
- Salt, to taste

1. Mix soy sauce, cornstarch, wine, and cumin in a bowl, and toss in lamb pieces.
2. Cover and marinate for 1 hour in the refrigerator.
3. Add oil and marinated lamb to a skillet then sear for minutes per side.
4. Mix chili peppers, Sichuan red pepper flakes, sugar, scallions, cilantro, salt, cumin seeds, and oil in a Cantonese wok.
5. Sauté for 1 minute, then add the seared lamb to the wok.
6. Continue cooking the lamb for 5 minutes.
7. Serve warm.

Pork, Red Peppers, Broccoli & Carrots Stir Fry

Prep time: 5 minutes | Cook time: 5 minutes| Serves 2

- 1/2 pound pork
  1 cup sliced red peppers
- 1 cup sliced broccoli
- 1/2 cup sliced carrots
- 1 tbsp. coconut oil

1. Marinade pork in a Superfoods marinade. Stir fry drained pork in coconut oil for few minutes, add broccoli and carrots and stir fry for 2 more minutes.
2. Add the rest of the marinade and red peppers and stir fry for a minute. Serve with brown rice or quinoa.

Xinjiang Lamb Rice

Prep time: 5 minutes | Cook time: 45 minutes| Serves 6

- 2 cups uncooked white rice
- 2 pounds fatty lamb, cut into chunks
- 4 cups water
- 3 ginger slices
- 3 tablespoons oil
- 1 medium onion, diced
- 2 teaspoons salt
- 2 teaspoons soy sauce
- 1 teaspoon cumin powder
- 1 pound carrots, cut into thin strips
- ¼ cup raisins

1. Sauté onion, ginger, and carrots with oil in a Mandarin wok for 5 minutes until soft.
2. Stir in lamb, salt, soy sauce, cumin powder then sautés for 8 minutes.
3. Add water to the lamb and bring it to a boil.
4. Stir in rice, cover, and cook for 15 minutes on medium-high heat.
5. Add raisins to the rice and mix well.
6. Cook for 5 minutes then serve warm.

Pork Fried Brown Rice

Prep time: 5 minutes | Cook time: 5 minutes| Serves 2

- 1/2 pound cubed pork
  1 cup peppers
- 1/2 cup sliced carrots
- 1 tbsp. black sesame seeds
- 1 cup cooked brown rice
- 1 tsp. oil

1. Marinade pork in a Superfoods marinade. Stir fry drained pork in coconut oil for few minutes, add all vegetables and stir fry for 2 more minutes.
2. Add the rest of the marinade and stir fry for a minute. Stir in brown rice and black sesame seeds.

Xi'an Cumin Lamb Burgers

Prep time: 5 minutes | Cook time: 15 minutes| Serves 4

- 1 tablespoon cumin seeds
- 1 teaspoon Sichuan peppercorns
- ½ teaspoon red chili flakes
- 1 pound ground lamb
- 1 teaspoon salt
- 1 medium red onion, sliced
- 1 jalapeno, thinly sliced
- 1 small red bell pepper, thinly sliced
- 1 tablespoon vegetable oil
- 1 cup plain Greek Yogurt
- 2 garlic cloves, minced
- 4 brioche or potato buns
- 1 cucumber, diced

1. Toast peppercorns, cumin seeds, and red chili flakes in a skillet.
2. Transfer the mixture to a pestle and grind with a mortar.
3. Mix the lamb with half of the toasted spice mixture and salt and make 4 patties out of it.
4. Set a wok with oil on medium heat and sear the patties for 2 minutes per side.
5. Transfer the patties to a plat and keep them covered aside.
6. Add peppers, and onion to the skillet until caramelize.
7. Mix yogurt with salt, garlic, and remaining spice mixture in a bowl.
8. Place one patty in each bun then divide caramelized onion, cucumber, and yogurt sauce in the burgers.
9. Serve.

Black Pepper Beef & Green Peppers Stir Fry

Prep time: 5 minutes | Cook time: 5 minutes| Serves 2

- 1/2 pound beef
  1 cup sliced green peppers
- 1 cup sliced onion
- 1/2 cup sliced celery
- 1 tbsp. coconut oil

1. Marinade beef in a Superfoods marinade. Stir fry drained beef in coconut oil for few minutes, add celery and onions and stir fry for 2 more minutes.
2. Add the rest of the marinade and green peppers and stir fry for a minute. Serve with brown rice or quinoa.

Pork, Carrots & Spinach Stir Fry

Prep time: 5 minutes | Cook time: 5 minutes| Serves 2

- 1/2 pound pork
  1 cup spinach
- 1 cup sliced carrots
- 1 Tbsp. coconut oil

1. Marinade pork in a Superfoods marinade. Stir fry drained pork in coconut oil for few minutes, add carrots and stir fry for 2 more minutes.
2. Add the rest of the marinade and spinach and stir fry for a minute. Serve with brown rice or quinoa.

Pork, Broccoli, Baby Carrots & Mushrooms Stir Fry

Prep time: 5 minutes | Cook time: 5 minutes| Serves 2

- 1/2 pound cubed pork
  1 cup sliced broccoli
- 1 cup halved lengthwise baby carrots
- 1/2 cup sliced mushrooms
- 1 tbsp. coconut oil

1. Marinade pork in a Superfoods marinade. Stir fry drained pork in coconut oil for few minutes, add broccoli and baby carrots and stir fry for 2 more minutes.
2. Add the rest of the marinade and mushrooms and stir fry for a minute. Serve with brown rice or quinoa.

Beef, Onions & Chili Stir Fry

Prep time: 5 minutes | Cook time: 5 minutes| Serves 2

- 1/2 pound beef
  1 cup sliced onions
- 1/2 cup sliced celery
- 1 Tbsp. coconut oil
- 1 Tsp. chili sauce (to taste)

1. Marinade pork in a Superfoods marinade with chili sauce added. Stir fry drained beef in coconut oil for few minutes, add onions and celery and stir fry for 2 more minutes.
2. Add the rest of the marinade and red peppers and stir fry for a minute. Serve with brown rice or quinoa.

Pork, Bok Choy & GreenPeppers Stir Fry

Prep time: 5 minutes | Cook time: 5 minutes| Serves 2

- 1/2 pound pork
  1 cup sliced green peppers
- 1 cup sliced bok choy
- 1/2 cup sliced green onions
- 1 tbsp. coconut oil

1. Marinade pork in a Superfoods marinade. Stir fry drained pork in coconut oil for few minutes, add white parts of bok choy and green onions and stir

fry for 2 more minutes.
2. Add the rest of the marinade and green peppers and the rest of bok choy and stir fry for a minute. Serve with brown rice or quinoa.

Lamb, Mushrooms & Broccoli Stir Fry

Prep time: 5 minutes | Cook time: 5 minutes| Serves 2

- 1/2 pound lamb
  1 cup sliced mushrooms
- 1 cup sliced broccoli
- 1/2 cup sliced onions
- 1 tbsp. coconut oil

1. Marinade lamb in a Superfoods marinade. Stir fry drained lamb in coconut oil for few minutes, add broccoli and onions and stir fry for 2 more minutes.
2. Add the rest of the marinade and mushrooms and stir fry for a minute. Serve with brown rice or quinoa.

Beef, Celery, Zucchini & Snow Peas Stir Fry

Prep time: 5 minutes | Cook time: 5 minutes| Serves 2

- 1/2 pound cubed beef
  1 cup sliced zucchini
- 1/2 cup sliced celery
- 1/2 cup sliced onions
- 1/2 cup sliced snow peas
- 1 Tsp. oil

1. Marinade beef in a Superfoods marinade. Stir fry drained beef in coconut oil for few minutes, add all vegetables and stir fry for 2 more minutes.
2. Add the rest of the marinade and stir fry for a minute. Serve with brown rice or quinoa.

Chicken, Green Beans & Broccoli Stir Fry

Prep time: 5 minutes | Cook time: 5 minutes| Serves 2

- 1/2 pound chicken
  1 cup sliced green beans
- 1 cup sliced broccoli
- 1/2 cup sliced Onions
- 1 Tbsp. oil

1. Marinade chicken in a Superfoods marinade. Stir fry drained chicken in coconut oil for few minutes, add all vegetables and stir fry for 2 more minutes.
2. Add the rest of the marinade and stir fry for a minute. Serve with brown rice or quinoa.

Beef, Zucchini & Yellow Peppers Stir Fry

Prep time: 5 minutes | Cook time: 5 minutes| Serves 2

- 1/2 pound beef
  1 cup sliced zucchini
- 1 cup sliced yellow peppers
- 1/2 cup sliced onions
- 1 tbsp. oil

1. Marinade beef in a Superfoods marinade. Stir fry drained beef in coconut oil for few minutes, add all vegetables and stir fry for 2 more minutes.
2. Add the rest of the marinade and stir fry for a minute. Serve with brown rice or quinoa.

Pork, Green Pepper and Tomato Stir Fry

Prep time: 5 minutes | Cook time: 5 minutes| Serves 2

- 1/2 pound cubed pork
  1 cup green peppers
- 1/2 cup sliced tomatoes
- 1 tsp. ground black pepper
- 1 tsp. oil

1. Marinade pork in a Superfoods marinade. Stir fry drained pork in coconut oil for few minutes, add all vegetables and stir fry for 2 more minutes.
2. Add the rest of the marinade and stir fry for a minute. Serve with brown rice or quinoa.

Cumin Beef & Spinach Stir Fry

Prep time: 5 minutes | Cook time: 5 minutes| Serves 2

- 1/2 pound beef
  1 cup sliced spinach
- 1 cup sliced chinese celery
- 1/2 cup sliced onions
- 1 tbsp. coconut oil
- 2 tsp. ground cumin

1. Marinade beef in a Superfoods marinade (add ground cumin). Stir fry drained beef in coconut oil for few minutes, add onions and Chinese celery and stir fry for 2 more minutes.
2. Add the rest of the marinade and spinach and stir fry for a minute. Serve with brown rice or quinoa.

Pork, Red & Green Peppers, Onion & Carrots Stir Fry

Prep time: 5 minutes | Cook time: 5 minutes| Serves 2

- 1/2 pound cubed pork
  1/2 cup chopped red peppers
- 1/2 cup chopped green peppers
- 1/2 cup sliced onion
- 1/2 cup sliced carrots
- 1 tsp. oil

1. Marinade pork in a Superfoods marinade. Stir fry drained pork in coconut oil for few minutes, add all vegetables and stir fry for 2 more minutes.
2. Add the rest of the marinade and stir fry for a minute. Serve with brown rice or quinoa.

Chicken & Sprouts Stir Fry

Prep time: 5 minutes | Cook time: 5 minutes| Serves 2

- 1/2 pound chicken
  2 cups sprouts
- 1 Tbsp. oil

1. Marinade chicken in a Superfoods marinade. Stir fry drained chicken in coconut oil for few minutes, add all vegetables and stir fry for 2 more minutes.
2. Add the rest of the marinade and stir fry for a minute. Serve with brown rice or quinoa.

Pork, Onions & Celery on Lettuce Stir Fry

Prep time: 5 minutes | Cook time: 5 minutes| Serves 2

- 1/2 pound pork, cubed
  2 cups sliced celery
- 1/2 cup sliced onions
- 1 tbsp. oil
- 2 cups lettuce leaves

1. Marinade pork in a Superfoods marinade. Stir fry drained pork in coconut oil for few minutes, add all vegetables and stir fry for 2 more minutes.
2. Add the rest of the marinade and stir fry for a minute. Serve over lettuce leaves.

Beef, Sprouts, Yellow Peppers & Snow Peas Stir Fry

Prep time: 5 minutes | Cook time: 5 minutes| Serves 2

- 1/2 pound beef
  1 cup sprouts
- 1 cup yellow peppers
- 1/2 cup snow peas
- 1 Tbsp. coconut oil

1. Marinade beef in a Superfoods marinade. Stir fry drained beef in coconut oil for few minutes, add yellow peppers and snow peas and stir fry for 2 more minutes.
2. Add sprouts and the rest of the marinade and stir fry for a minute. Serve with brown rice or quinoa.

Chinese Braised Lamb Casserole

Prep time: 5 minutes | Cook time: 1 hour, 10 minutes | Serves 6

- 2½ pounds lamb breast, cut into 2-inch pieces
- 15 ginger slices
- 2 tablespoons oil
- 6 scallions
- 10 grams rock sugar
- 3 pieces fermented red bean curd
- ¼ cup Zhu Hou sauce
- 1-star anise
- 3 tablespoons Shaoxing wine
- 1 teaspoon dark soy sauce
- 2 tablespoons light soy sauce
- 2 tablespoons oyster sauce
- 1 dried tangerine peel
- 6 dried Shiitake mushrooms, soaked and cut in half
- 4 small carrots, cut into chunks
- 1 small bamboo shoot, peeled and cut into slices
- 6 bean thread/sticks, soaked and cut into large chunks
- Salt, to taste

1. Add lamb and 4 slices of ginger to a cooking pan and fill it with water.
2. Boil the lamb then drain and rinse under cold water.
3. Sauté ginger, and scallions with 2 tablespoons oil in a Cantonese wok.
4. Stir in sugar, red bean curd, and Zha Hou sauce, then cook for 5 minutes.
5. Add lamb, star anise, wine, soy sauces, oyster sauce, mushroom water, mushrooms, peel, and enough water to cover all the ingredients.
6. Cover and cook the lamb mixture for 60 minutes.
7. Add bamboo shoots, bean threads, and carrot, then cook for 20 minutes.
8. Serve warm.

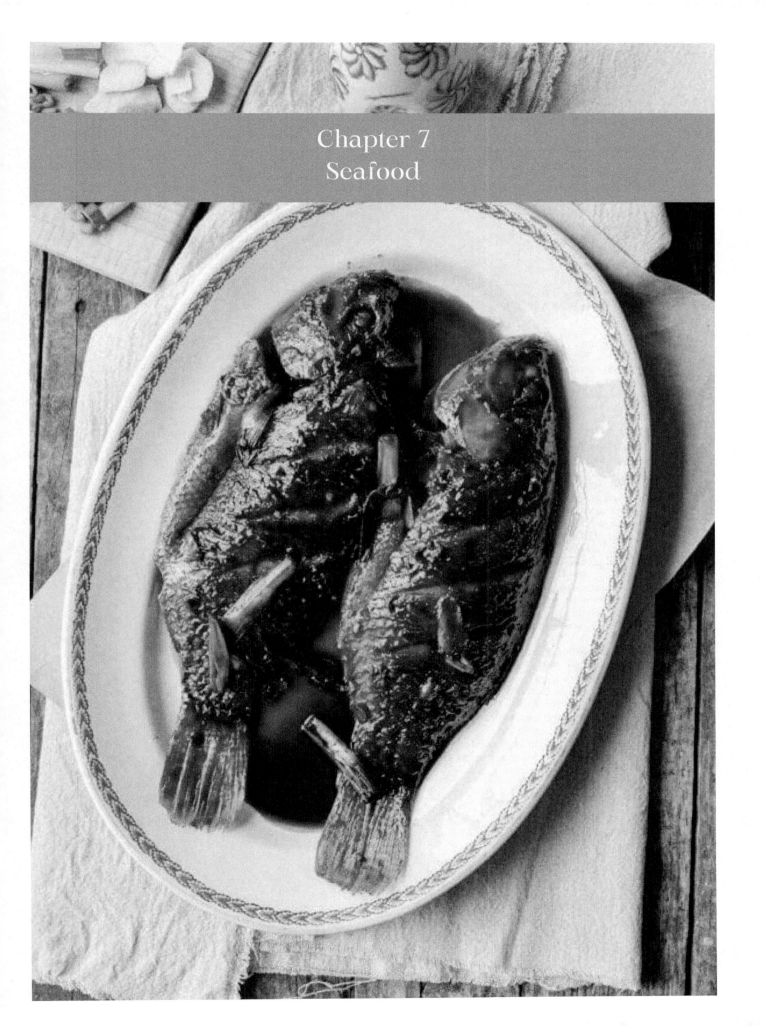

Chapter 7
Seafood

Steamed Mussels

Prep time: 5 minutes | Cook time: 15 minutes| Serves 4

- 3 pounds mussels, debearded
- Sliced rustic bread
- 2 tablespoons olive oil
- 4 garlic cloves, chopped
- 2 sprigs fresh thyme
- ½ cup onion, chopped
- ¼ teaspoon salt
- ½ cup broth
- ¼ teaspoon sugar
- ⅓ cup dry white wine
- ¼ cup fresh parsley, chopped
- Black pepper

1. Sauté onion, with olive oil, garlic, and thyme in a Mandarin wok until soft.
2. Stir in white wine, broth, black pepper, and mussels.
3. Reduce its heat to low, cover, and cook the mussels for 6–7 minutes.
4. Serve warm.

Hunan-Style Fish

Prep time: 5 minutes | Cook time: 50 minutes| Serves 3

- 1 ½ pounds fresh tilapia
- 16 ounces silken tofu
- ⅛ teaspoon salt
- 3 tablespoons canola oil
- 1 ½ tablespoons ginger, minced
- 6 tablespoons Duo Jiao
- 3 garlic cloves, minced
- 1 scallion, diced
- ⅔ cup hot water
- 2 tablespoons soy sauce
- 1 teaspoon sugar
- ¼ teaspoon white pepper

1. Mix hot water, soy sauce, sugar, white pepper, garlic, ginger, salt, scallions, and Duo Jiao in a Mandarin wok.
2. Cook this sauce until the sauce is reduced to half, then allow it to cool.
3. Soak the tofu and fillets in the prepared sauce, rub well, and cover to marinate for 30 minutes.
4. Add oil to a cooking pan and place it over medium heat.
5. Sear the tofu and fish in the skillet for 5 minutes per side until golden-brown.
6. Serve warm.

Chinese Shrimp Cakes

Prep time: 5 minutes | Cook time: 15 minutes| Serves 4

- 1 pound shrimp, chopped
- 1 small carrot, blanched and chopped
- 5 water chestnuts, minced
- ¼ cup cilantro, finely chopped
- 1 teaspoon ginger, grated
- 2 teaspoons Shaoxing wine
- ½ teaspoon salt
- 1/8 teaspoon ground white pepper
- 2 teaspoons oyster sauce
- 1 teaspoon sesame oil
- ¼ teaspoon sugar
- 1 teaspoon cornstarch
- 3 tablespoons oil

1. Mix water chestnuts, shrimp, carrot, ginger, cilantro, wine, white, and rest of the Prep time: 5 minutes | Cook time: 5 minutes| Serves 4(except oil) in a bowl.
2. Add oil to a Cantonese wok and place it over medium-high heat.
3. Make 10 patties out of this mixture and sear the patties in batches in the skillet.
4. Cook the patties for 5 minutes per side until golden-brown.
5. Serve warm.

Typhoon Shelter Shrimp

Prep time: 5 minutes | Cook time: 15 minutes| Serves 4

- 1 pound large, head-on shrimp
- ¼ teaspoon white pepper powder
- 2 teaspoons Shaoxing wine
- 3-4 ginger slices, minced
- 7 garlic cloves, minced
- 2 scallions, chopped
- 3 red chilies, chopped
- 1 cup panko breadcrumbs
- 1 cup vegetable oil
- ½ teaspoon salt
- ¼ teaspoon sugar
- 1/8 teaspoon five-spice powder

1. Sauté ginger and garlic with vegetable oil in a Mandarin wok until golden-brown.
2. Stir in white pepper, wine, red chilies, scallions, salt, sugar, and spice powder.
3. Mix and toss in shrimp, then cook for 5–6 minutes.
4. Spread the shrimp in a baking dish and drizzle the panko crumbs on top.
5. Bake the shrimp for 2 minutes in the oven at 350°F.
6. Serve warm.

Shrimp and Broccoli with Brown Sauce

Prep time: 5 minutes | Cook time: 15 minutes| Serves 6

- 16 shrimps; peeled, deveined, and butterflied
- 10 ounces broccoli florets
- ½ cup chicken stock
- ¼ teaspoon granulated sugar
- 1 ½ tablespoons soy sauce
- ½ teaspoon dark soy sauce
- 1 tablespoon oyster sauce
- ½ teaspoon sesame oil
- 1/8 teaspoon white pepper
- 2 tablespoons canola oil
- 2 garlic cloves, chopped
- 1 tablespoon Shaoxing wine
- 1 ½ tablespoons cornstarch, whisked with 2 tablespoons water

1. Add sesame oil to a large wok and stir in garlic.
2. Sauté until the garlic turns golden, then add broccoli.
3. Stir and cook for 5 minutes until soft.
4. Add shrimp, sugar, soy sauce, chicken stock, oyster sauce, white pepper, and wine to the saucepan.
5. Cook the mixture until the shrimp are tender.
6. Stir in cornstarch, mix and cook until the mixture thickens.
7. Serve warm.

Squid, Shrimp, Celery & Bitter Gourd Stir Fry

Prep time: 5 minutes | Cook time: 5 minutes| Serves 2

- 1/4 pound shrimp
- 1/4 pound squid
  1 cup sliced celery
- 1/2 cup sliced bitter gourd
- 1 tbsp. coconut oil

1. Marinade shrimp and squid in a Superfoods marinade. Stir fry drained shrimp and squid in coconut oil for few minutes, add celery and biter gourd and stir fry for 2 more minutes.
2. Add the rest of the marinade and stir fry for a minute. Serve with brown rice or quinoa.

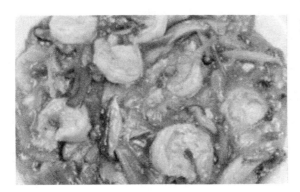

Baby Octopus, Green Peppers & Carrot Stir Fry

Prep time: 5 minutes | Cook time: 5 minutes| Serves 2

- 1/2 pound baby octopus
  1 cup sliced green peppers
- 1/2 cup sliced carrots
- 2 sliced green onions
- 1/2 cup cashews
- 1 Tsp. oil

1. Marinade octopus in a Superfoods marinade. Stir fry drained octopus in coconut oil for few minutes, add all vegetables and stir fry for 2 more minutes.
2. Add the rest of the marinade and stir fry for a minute. Serve with brown rice or quinoa.

Fish, Sprouts, Chinese Celery & Dill Stir Fry

Prep time: 5 minutes | Cook time: 5 minutes| Serves 2

- 1/2 pound fish of your choice
  2 cups sprouts
- 2 cup sliced chinese celery
- 1/2 cup sliced dill
- 1 tbsp. coconut oil

1. Marinade fish in a Superfoods marinade. Stir fry drained fish in coconut oil for few minutes, add all vegetables and stir fry for 2 more minutes.
2. Add the rest of the marinade and stir fry for a minute. Serve with brown rice or quinoa.

Shrimp, Celery & Garlic Stir Fry

Prep time: 5 minutes | Cook time: 5 minutes| Serves 2

- 1/2 pound shrimp
  1 + 1/2 cup sliced celery
- 2 minced garlic cloves
- 1 tbsp. coconut oil

1. Marinade shrimp in a Superfoods marinade. Stir fry drained shrimp in coconut oil for few minutes, add celery and garlic and stir fry for 2 more minutes.
2. Add the rest of the marinade and stir fry for a minute. Serve with brown rice or quinoa.

Octopus, Green Peppers & Mushrooms Stir Fry

Prep time: 5 minutes | Cook time: 5 minutes| Serves 2

- 1/2 pound cubed octopus
  1 cup sliced green peppers
- 1/2 cup sliced celery
- 1/2 cup sliced onions
- 1/2 cup sliced mushrooms
- 1 Tsp. oil

1. Marinade octopus in a Superfoods marinade. Stir fry drained octopus in coconut oil for few minutes, add all vegetables and stir fry for 2 more minutes.
2. Add the rest of the marinade and stir fry for a minute. Serve with brown rice or quinoa.

Bitter Gourd, Shrimp & Squid Stir Fry

Prep time: 5 minutes | Cook time: 5 minutes| Serves 2

- 1/2 pound squid slices
  1/2 pound shrimp
- 1 cup sliced bitter gourd
- 1/2 cup sliced onions
- 1 tbsp. coconut oil

1. Marinade shrimp and squid in a Superfoods marinade. Stir fry drained shrimp and squid in coconut oil for few minutes, add bitter gourd and stir fry for 2 more minutes.
2. Add the rest of the marinade and onions and stir fry for a minute. Serve with brown rice or quinoa.

Spicy Squid, Zucchini & Celery Stir Fry

Prep time: 5 minutes | Cook time: 5 minutes| Serves 2

- 1/2 pound squid
  1/2 cup sliced zucchini
- 1 + 1/2 cup sliced celery
- 1/2 cup sliced onions
- 1 tbsp. coconut oil
- 1 tbsp. chili powder (to taste)

1. Marinade squid in a Superfoods marinade. Stir fry drained squid in coconut oil for few minutes, add all veggies and stir fry for 2 more minutes.
2. Add the rest of the marinade and stir fry for a minute. Serve with brown rice or quinoa.

Salmon With Parsley Sauce

Prep time: 5 minutes | Cook time: 20 minutes| Serves 4

- 1 (1½-pound) wild salmon fillet
- 4 teaspoons extra-virgin olive oil, divided
- Sea salt
- Ground black pepper
- 1 cup fresh flat-leaf parsley leaves
- 1 medium garlic clove, peeled
- 2 scallions, cut into 1-inch pieces
- 2 teaspoons capers

1. Preheat the oven to 200°F. Line a rimmed baking sheet with parchment paper or aluminum foil.
2. Place the salmon fillet on the baking sheet. Rub 1 teaspoon of the oil on the top of the fillet. Season with salt and pepper to taste.
3. Bake for 20 minutes, then check for doneness by flaking the center with a fork—it should be medium-rare. If it's not done yet, put it back in the oven and continue to check it every 5 minutes.
4. Meanwhile, combine the parsley, garlic, scallions, and capers in a food processor and pulse about 10 times, until the mixture is chopped but not completely smooth.
5. Add 2 teaspoons of the oil and process just until combined.
6. Transfer the parsley sauce to a small bowl and drizzle in as much of the remaining 1 teaspoon of oil as you like.
7. Remove the salmon from the oven, put it on a platter, and top with the parsley sauce. Feel free to drizzle with more olive oil. Enjoy!

Roasted Blood Orange Salmon

Prep time: 5 minutes | Cook time: 15 minutes| Serves 4

- 1 tablespoon coconut sugar or brown sugar
- 1 blood orange, zested, peeled, and sliced
- ½ teaspoon five-spice powder
- ¼ teaspoon sea salt
- ⅛ teaspoon freshly ground black pepper
- 1 (1½-pound) skinless wild salmon fillet, cut into 4 pieces
- 1½ tablespoons Dijon mustard
- 2 tablespoons chopped fresh cilantro, for garnish

1. Preheat the oven to 450°F. Line a rimmed baking sheet with parchment paper.
2. In a small bowl, combine the sugar, orange zest, five-spice powder, salt, and pepper.
3. Place the salmon on the baking sheet. Spread the Dijon mustard evenly on top of the salmon. Sprinkle the sugar-orange mixture evenly over the mustard.
4. Bake until the salmon is cooked to your liking, about 15 minutes.
5. Garnish with cilantro and orange slices. Enjoy!

Baby Carrots & Shrimp Stir Fry

Prep time: 5 minutes | Cook time: 5 minutes| Serves 2

- 1/2 pound shrimp
  1 cup baby carrots
- 1/2 cup sliced Broccoli
- 1/2 cup sliced mushrooms
- 1 Tbsp. coconut oil

1. Marinade pork in a Superfoods marinade. Stir fry drained shrimp in coconut oil for few minutes, add broccoli and carrots and stir fry for 2 more minutes.
2. Add the rest of the marinade and mushrooms and stir fry for a minute. Serve with brown rice or quinoa.

Shrimp Toast

Prep time: 10 minutes | Cook time: 5 minutes | Serves 4

- 8 ounces shrimp, cooked and peeled
- 2 cloves garlic, crushed
- 1 tablespoon soy sauce
- 1 teaspoon sesame oil
- 1 large egg
- 4 slices white bread, crusts removed
- 1 tablespoon sesame seeds, toasted
- 2 tablespoons vegetable oil
- Sweet and sour sauce, to use as dip

1. Use a blender or food processor to puree the shrimp and garlic.
2. Add the soy sauce, sesame oil, and egg. Pulse or process a little longer until paste-like in consistency.
3. Spread the paste on the bread slices.
4. Sprinkle with sesame seeds. Press down on the sesame seeds with a spatula or the back of a spoon so they stick to the paste.
5. Heat the oil in a skillet over medium heat.
6. Cut the bread into small triangles, and fry them with the spread side up until golden brown, about 3-4 minutes.
7. Drain on a cooling rack or a plate lined with paper towels.
8. Serve with sweet and sour sauce.

Chapter 8
Vegetables

Vegan General Tso's "Chicken"

Prep time: 15 minutes | Cook time: 25 minutes| Serves 8

SAUCE

- 1/3 cup Asian vegetable stock
- 1 teaspoon dark soy sauce
- 1 tablespoon soy sauce
- 2 teaspoons rice vinegar
- 1 teaspoon Shaoxing wine
- 3 ½ tablespoons brown sugar
- ¼ teaspoon white pepper

FOR THE DISH

- 1 pound cauliflower floret
- 2 cups broccoli florets
- 1 tablespoon vegetable oil
- 4–5 dried red chili peppers
- 3 garlic cloves, minced
- 1 tablespoon cornstarch, whisked with 2 tablespoons water

1. Mix all the sauce ingredients in a bowl and set it aside.
2. Saute cauliflower, broccoli, and garlic with oil in a Cantonese wok for 5 minutes.
3. Pour in sauce and add cornstarch then mix well.
4. Cover and cook for 10 minutes on medium-low heat.
5. Serve warm.

Spicy Dry-Fried String Beans

Prep time: 5 minutes | Cook time: 5 minutes| Serves: 4

FOR THE SAUCE

1 tablespoon Shaoxing wine
1 teaspoon chili bean sauce
1 teaspoon sesame oil
1 teaspoon sugar
½ teaspoon salt

FOR THE STRING BEANS

1 tablespoon peanut oil
1 pound fresh string beans, trimmed
8 dried red chile peppers
½-inch piece ginger, peeled and julienned
3 garlic cloves, minced

1. In a small bowl, prepare the sauce by mixing together the Shaoxing wine, chili bean sauce, sesame oil, sugar, and salt. Set it aside.
2. In a wok over medium-high heat, heat the peanut oil.
3. As soon as the wok starts to smoke, toss in the green beans. Stir-fry until they are blistered and bright green, for about 5 minutes. If they start to burn, reduce the heat to medium.
4. Add the dried red chiles, ginger, and garlic to the wok. Fry until aromatic, then add the sauce. Stir to combine all the ingredients.
5. Remove from the heat, and transfer to a serving plate.

Marinated Roasted Beets

Prep time: 10 minutes | Cook time: 25 minutes| Serves 6

- 1 ½ pounds beets, peeled and cut into ¼-inch circles
- Olive oil, for cooking
- 1–3 garlic cloves, minced
- 1 teaspoon honey
- 1 tablespoon Chinese black vinegar
- Salt and black pepper, to taste
- Fresh herbs, for garnish

1. Toss beets with olive oil in a baking tray.
2. Roast the beets for 20 minutes in the oven at 400°F.
3. Mix honey with garlic, 2 tablespoons olive oil, black vinegar, black pepper, salt, and herbs in a Mandarin wok.
4. Toss in roasted beets and sauté for 5 minutes.
5. Serve warm.

Spicy Oyster Mushroom

Prep time: 5 minutes | Cook time: 25 minutes| Serves 6

- 1 pound king oyster mushrooms
- 5 tablespoons vegetable oil
- 6 ginger slices
- 8 garlic cloves, sliced
- 1 tablespoon spicy bean sauce
- 1 tablespoon light soy sauce
- ½ teaspoon sugar
- 5 long hot peppers, sliced diagonally

1. Sauté mushrooms, ginger, and garlic with oil in a Cantonese wok for 5 minutes.
2. Stir in bean sauce, soy sauce, sugar, and hot peppers.
3. Mix well and cover to cook for 5 minutes on low heat.
4. Serve warm.

Stir-Fried Spinach with Garlic

Prep time: 5 minutes | Cook time: 5 minutes| Serves: 4

- 1 tablespoon olive oil
- 4 garlic cloves, thinly sliced or minced
- 6 cups fresh spinach, rinsed
- Pinch salt
- ½ teaspoon chicken stock granules

1. In a wok over medium-high heat, heat the olive oil.
2. Add the garlic, and stir-fry until aromatic, just a few seconds.
3. Toss in the spinach, salt, and chicken stock granules.
4. Stir-fry the spinach until the leaves wilt.
5. Transfer to a serving dish.

Spicy Garlic Eggplant

Prep time: 10 minutes | Cook time: 10 minutes| Serves: 4

FOR THE SAUCE

- 2 tablespoons soy sauce
- 1½ tablespoons Chinese black vinegar or apple cider vinegar
- 1 teaspoon dark soy sauce
- 1½ teaspoons brown sugar
- 2 teaspoons chili bean paste

FOR THE STIR-FRY

- 2 Chinese or Japanese eggplant, cut into bite-size pieces
- 1 teaspoon cornstarch
- 3 tablespoons peanut oil
- 4 garlic cloves, minced
- 1 scallion, chopped

1. In a small bowl, prepare the sauce by mixing together the soy sauce, vinegar, dark soy sauce, brown sugar, and chili bean paste. Set it aside.
2. Dust the eggplant with a light layer of cornstarch.
3. In a wok over medium-high heat, heat the peanut oil.
4. Stir-fry the eggplant until cooked almost all the way through.
5. Add the garlic and stir-fry until aromatic.
6. Add the sauce to the wok, stir-frying until all the ingredients are mixed, then remove from the heat.
7. Transfer the eggplant to a serving dish, and garnish with the chopped scallion.

Chinese Cucumber Salad

Prep time: 5 minutes | Cook time: 5 minutes| Serves 4

- 6 garlic cloves, minced
- 3 tablespoons oil
- 2 English cucumbers, sliced
- 1½ teaspoon salt
- 1 teaspoon sugar
- 1/8 teaspoon MSG
- ¼ teaspoon sesame oil
- 1 tablespoon rice vinegar

1. Sauté garlic with oil in a Cantonese wok for 30 seconds.
2. Stir in sugar, MSG, sesame oil, rice vinegar, and salt.
3. Cook for 1 minute, then toss in cucumber.
4. Mix well and serve.

Broccoli with Braised Shiitake Mushrooms

Prep time: 10 Minutes, Plus 30 Minutes For Soaking | Cook time: 20 minutes| Serves: 6

- 2 cups dried shiitake
- mushrooms
- Water for soaking mushrooms
- FOR THE SAUCE
- ¼ cup water, plus 2 tablespoons for cornstarch mixture
- ¼ cup oyster sauce
- 1 tablespoon soy sauce
- 1 teaspoon sugar
- 2 pinches ground white pepper
- 2 teaspoons cornstarch
- FOR THE BROCCOLI
- 2 heads broccoli, cut into florets
- 1 tablespoon peanut oil
- 1 tablespoon sesame oil

1. Soak the shiitake mushrooms in water for a few hours or overnight until soft. If pressed for time, boil them in water for 30 minutes.
2. Rinse the mushrooms well, remove their stems, and squeeze as much water out of them as possible. Set them aside.
3. In a small bowl, prepare the sauce by combining ¼ cup of water and the oyster sauce, soy sauce, sugar, and pepper. Set it aside.
4. In another small bowl, combine 2 tablespoons of water and the cornstarch. Set it aside.
5. On a metal steaming rack in a wok over high heat, steam the broccoli florets for 5 minutes. Set them aside, and discard the water from the wok.
6. Return the wok to the stove top. Allow the wok to dry completely. Over medium-low heat, heat the peanut oil and sesame oil.
7. Add the sauce and mushrooms to the wok. Simmer for about 10 minutes, stirring occasionally.
8. Increase the heat to high, and add the cornstarch-water mixture, stirring to thicken the sauce.
9. Put the broccoli on a round serving plate in a circle along the edge. Pour the mushrooms and sauce in the center of the plate, and serve.

Happy Family

Prep time: 5 Minutes, Plus 20 Minutes To Marinate | Cook time: 30 minutes| Serves: 6

- 1 cup thin strips chicken breast
- 2 teaspoons soy sauce
- 2 teaspoons cornstarch
- 2 tablespoons peanut oil
- 6 to 8 large shrimp
- 2 garlic cloves, minced
- 2 cups broccoli florets
- 1 carrot, sliced
- 1 cup snow peas, trimmed
- 1 cup baby corn
- 1 cup sliced button mushrooms
- ¼ cup bamboo shoots
- ¼ cup water chestnuts, sliced
- 1 cup Brown Sauce

1. Marinate the chicken breast strips in the soy sauce and cornstarch for 20 minutes at room temperature.
2. In a wok over medium-high heat, heat the peanut oil.
3. Add the chicken and stir-fry until cooked, then remove the chicken from the wok.
4. Add the shrimp and stir-fry until they are pink and opaque, then remove them from the wok.
5. Toss the garlic into the wok and add the vegetables one by one, stir-frying each for 20 to 30 seconds before adding the next vegetable. Begin with the broccoli, followed by the carrot, snow peas, baby corn, mushrooms, bamboo shoots, and water chestnuts.
6. Return the chicken and shrimp to the wok.
7. Pour in the brown sauce and stir all the ingredients well. As soon as the sauce has thickened, turn off the heat and transfer to a serving plate.

Steamed Seitan with Mushrooms

Prep time: 5 minutes | Cook time: 5 minutes| Serves 4

- 1/3 cup dried wood ear mushrooms, soaked
- ½ cup dried lily flowers, soaked
- 4 large dried shiitake mushrooms, soaked
- 1½ cups seitan, cut into bite-sized pieces
- ½ cup mushroom soaking liquid
- 1 tablespoon vegetable oil
- ½ teaspoon sesame oil
- 1 tablespoon Shaoxing wine
- 1 tablespoon oyster sauce
- ½ teaspoon sugar
- ¾ teaspoon salt
- ¼ teaspoon white pepper
- 1 teaspoon ginger, grated
- 1 scallion, chopped
- 1½ tablespoons cornstarch

1. Drain the mushrooms, lily flowers, and wood ears, and transfer to a wok.
2. Add ginger, oil, soaking liquid, oyster sauce, sugar, salt, white pepper, and white part of scallions.

3. Cook until the liquid is absorbed then add green parts of scallions.
4. Stir and cook for 30 seconds then add cornstarch, seitan, and rest of the ingredients.
5. Mix well, cover, and cook for 15 minutes on medium-low heat.
6. Serve warm.

Kale with Tomatoes and Adzuki Beans

Prep time: 5 minutes | Cook time: 10 minutes| Serves 4

- 2 tablespoons extra-virgin olive oil, divided
- 1 pint grape tomatoes
- 3 tablespoons balsamic vinegar
- 2 bunches lacinato (black) kale (about 1 pound total), thick center ribs removed and discarded, leaves cut into 2-inch pieces
- 1 (15-ounce) can adzuki beans, rinsed and drained
- Sea salt
- Freshly ground black pepper
- ½ cup shredded vegan or regular Parmesan cheese

1. Heat 1 tablespoon of the oil in a large skillet over medium heat. Add the tomatoes and cook, stirring occasionally, until they blister and start to blacken a bit, about 10 minutes.
2. Add the vinegar, kale, and beans. Cook, stirring, until the kale just wilts, about 30 seconds.
3. Transfer the mixture to a large bowl. Season with salt and pepper to taste. Stir in the Parmesan and enjoy!

Chopped Broccoli Salad

Prep time: 10 minutes| Serves 4

- 4 cups broccoli florets, chopped
- 2 scallions, sliced
- ⅓ cup unsweetened dried tart cherries
- ¼ cup raw almonds, chopped
- ¼ cup longan fruit (long yan rou), chopped
- 2 tablespoons raw sunflower seeds
- 3 tablespoons mayonnaise (I like to use an avocado oil–based one)
- 2 teaspoons raw apple cider vinegar
- 1 tablespoon coconut, granulated, or brown sugar

1. In a large bowl, toss together the chopped broccoli, scallions, cherries, almonds, longan fruit, and sunflower seeds.
2. In a small bowl, whisk together the mayonnaise, vinegar, and sugar.
3. Add as much dressing as you like to the salad. Toss to combine, and enjoy!

Penne with Arugula Pesto

Prep time: 10 minutes | Serves 4

- 12 ounces chickpea penne or regular penne, cooked to al dente and drained (Note: Reserve about ⅓ cup of the pasta cooking water in case you need it to thin out your pesto.)
- 2 cups arugula
- 3 tablespoons extra-virgin olive oil
- Grated zest and juice of 1 lemon
- ½ cup raw cashews
- 2 garlic cloves, peeled
- 2 tablespoons shredded vegan or regular Parmesan cheese
- Pinch red pepper flakes
- Sea salt

1. Put the cooked pasta in a large bowl and set it aside.
2. In a food processor, combine the arugula, oil, lemon zest and juice, cashews, garlic, Parmesan, red pepper flakes, and salt to taste. Process until finely minced.
3. Add as much of the reserved pasta cooking water as you need to achieve a creamy pesto consistency.
4. Toss the pesto with the pasta and enjoy!

Unstuffed Cabbage

Prep time: 5 minutes | Cook time: 40 minutes | Serves 4

- 2 tablespoons ghee or unsalted butter
- 1 medium onion, chopped
- 3 garlic cloves, chopped
- 1¼ pounds ground beef
- Sea salt
- Ground black pepper
- 3 tablespoons chopped fresh dill
- 1 tablespoon chopped fresh oregano
- 1 teaspoon ground turmeric
- 1 teaspoon caraway seeds (optional)
- 1 teaspoon coconut, granulated, or brown sugar
- 1 (28-ounce) can crushed tomatoes
- 1 tablespoon balsamic vinegar
- 3 large collard green leaves, center ribs removed and discarded, leaves cut into 2-inch squares
- ½ head green cabbage, leaves separated and cut into 2-inch squares

1. In a large pot, melt the ghee over medium heat. Add the onion, garlic, and beef. Season with salt and pepper to taste.
2. Cook, using a spoon to stir and break up the meat, until the meat is no longer pink.
3. Stir in the dill, oregano, turmeric, caraway seeds (if using), and sugar and cook for 5 minutes.
4. Stir in the tomatoes and vinegar and cook for an additional 15 minutes.
5. Add the collards and cabbage and stir gently until the leaves are coated with the sauce. Cook just until the leaves are slightly softened, about 10 minutes.
6. Ladle into shallow bowls and enjoy!

Chapter 9
Noodle and Rice Dishes

Beef Chow Fun (Gon Chow Ngo Ho)

Prep time: 15 minutes | Cook time: 10 minutes | Serves 4

- ¼ cup Shaoxing cooking wine
- ¼ cup light soy sauce
- 2 tablespoons cornstarch
- 1½ tablespoons dark soy sauce
- ½ teaspoon sugar
- Ground white pepper
- 12 ounces flank steak or sirloin tips, cut across the grain into ⅛-inch-thick slices
- 1½ pounds fresh, wide rice noodles or ¾ pound dried
- 2 tablespoons sesame oil, divided
- 3 tablespoons cooking oil, divided
- 4 peeled fresh ginger slices, each about the size of a quarter
- Kosher salt
- 8 scallions, both white and green parts, halved lengthwise and cut into 3-inch pieces
- 1 cup fresh mung bean sprouts

1. In a mixing bowl, stir together the wine, light soy sauce, cornstarch, dark soy sauce, sugar, and a pinch of white pepper. Add the beef and toss to coat. Set aside to marinate for at least 10 minutes.
2. Bring a large pot of water to a boil and cook the rice noodles according to package instructions. Reserve 1 cup of the cooking water and drain the rest. Rinse the noodles with cold water and drizzle with 1 tablespoon of sesame oil. Set aside.
3. In the wok, heat 2 tablespoons of cooking oil over medium-high heat until it shimmers. Season the oil by adding the ginger and a pinch of salt. Allow the ginger to sizzle in the oil for about 30 seconds, swirling gently.
4. Using tongs, add the beef, reserving the marinating liquid. Sear the beef against the wok for 2 or 3 minutes, or until a brown crust develops. Toss and flip the beef around the wok for 1 more minute. Transfer to a clean bowl and set aside.
5. Add the remaining 1 tablespoon of cooking oil and stir-fry the scallions for 30 seconds, or until soft. Add the noodles and lift in a scooping upward motion to help separate the noodles if they have stuck together. Add the reserved cooking water, 1 tablespoon at a time, if the noodles have really glued themselves together.
6. Return the beef to the wok and toss to combine with the noodles. Pour in the reserved marinade and toss for 30 seconds to 1 minute, or until the sauce thickens and coats the noodles. They should turn a deep, rich brown color. If you need to, add 1 tablespoon of the reserved cooking water to thin out the sauce. Add the bean sprouts and toss until just heated through, about 1 minute. Remove the ginger and discard.
7. Transfer to a platter and drizzle with the remaining 1 tablespoon of sesame oil. Serve hot.

Ants Climbing A Tree (Ma Yi Shang Shu)

Prep time: 15 minutes | Cook time: 5 minutes | Serves 4

- 4 ounces rice stick noodles
- 1 teaspoon sesame oil
- 2 tablespoons cooking oil, divided
- 1 teaspoon chopped fresh ginger, minced
- 1 teaspoon garlic, crushed and chopped
- 2 teaspoons doubanjiang (Chinese chili bean paste)
- 4 ounces ground lean pork
- ¼ teaspoon freshly ground black pepper
- 1 teaspoon Shaoxing cooking wine
- 1 teaspoon light soy sauce
- 1 teaspoon dark soy sauce
- ½ teaspoon sugar
- 1 cup chicken broth
- Sea salt
- 1 teaspoon finely chopped red bell pepper, for garnishing
- 1 scallion, finely chopped, for garnishing

1. In a large bowl, soak the rice noodles in warm water for 15 minutes, or until soft. Drain the noodles and toss with the sesame oil to keep separated. Discard the water.
2. In the wok, heat the cooking oil over high heat until it shimmers. Add the ginger and garlic, and stir-fry until fragrant, about 10 seconds. Add the doubanjiang and stir-fry for about 1 minute, until fiery and blended.
3. Add the ground pork and stir-fry until it separates into bits. Add the black pepper, wine, light and dark soy sauces, sugar, and broth, and bring to a simmer. Add the noodles and stir occasionally until most of the broth has evaporated. Season with salt.
4. Garnish with the bell pepper and scallion greens.

Vegetarian Fried Rice (Sucai Chow Fan)

Prep time: 10 minutes | Cook time: 5 minutes | Serves 4

- 2 cups leftover cooked rice, at room temperature
- 1 tablespoon toasted sesame oil
- 1 tablespoon light soy sauce
- ½ teaspoon ground white pepper
- 2 tablespoons cooking oil
- 1 tablespoon chopped fresh ginger
- 2 garlic cloves, crushed and chopped
- 3 large eggs, beaten
- 1 medium onion, diced into ½-inch pieces
- 4 ounces sliced mushrooms
- 1 medium red bell pepper, diced into ½-inch pieces
- ½ cup frozen corn, thawed
- ½ cup frozen peas, thawed
- 4 scallions, both white and green parts, sliced into ¼-inch pieces

1. In a large bowl, combine the rice, sesame oil, soy sauce, and white pepper. Mix well.
2. In the wok, heat the cooking oil over high heat until it shimmers.
3. Add the ginger, garlic, and eggs and stir-fry for about 2 minutes, until the eggs are firm.
4. Add the onion, mushrooms, and bell pepper and stir-fry for 1 minute to mix well.
5. Add the corn and peas and stir-fry for 1 minute, until the peas are bright green.
6. Add the rice and scallions and stir-fry for 1 minute to mix and heat through. Serve.

Dan Dan Noodles (Dan Dan Mein)

Prep time: 15 minutes | Cook time: 15 minutes | Serves 4 to 6

- 1 pound fresh Chinese egg noodles (or about 8 ounces dried noodles), cooked according to package instructions
- 1 tablespoon, plus 2 teaspoons cooking oil, divided
- ½-inch piece fresh ginger, julienned
- 4 garlic cloves, crushed and chopped, divided
- 8 ounces ground pork
- 4 teaspoons light soy sauce, divided
- 1 teaspoon dark soy sauce
- ½ teaspoon brown sugar
- ½ teaspoon salt
- 1 teaspoon ground Sichuan peppercorns
- ½ cup chicken broth
- 2 teaspoons rice vinegar
- Pinch salt
- Pinch ground white pepper
- 1 scallion, both white and green parts, chopped, for garnishing
- ¼ cup unsalted roasted peanuts, chopped, for garnishing

1. Rinse the prepared noodles under cold tap water. Make sure most of the water is drained, then divide the noodles evenly among 4 serving bowls.
2. In the wok, heat 2 teaspoons of oil over medium heat until it shimmers. Add the ginger and half of the garlic and stir-fry for about 20 seconds, until aromatic.
3. Add the ground pork and stir-fry for 2 minutes, until fully cooked. Add 2 teaspoons of light soy sauce and the dark soy sauce, brown sugar, salt, and pepper, mixing to combine. Distribute this pork mixture evenly among the serving bowls, sprinkled over the noodles.
4. Add the remaining 1 tablespoon of oil, the Sichuan peppercorns, and the remaining 2 garlic cloves to the wok, and stir-fry for about 20 seconds.
5. Add the chicken broth, rice vinegar, remaining 2 teaspoons of soy sauce, salt, and white pepper, then stir to combine. Remove from the heat and divide the broth evenly over the pork in each serving bowl.
6. Garnish each bowl with the chopped scallion and peanuts.

Crossing The Bridge Noodles (Guoqiao Mixian)

Prep time: 10 minutes | Cook time: 10 minutes | Serves 4

- 2 tablespoons cooking oil
- 1 tablespoon chopped fresh ginger
- 3 garlic cloves, crushed and chopped
- 4 ounces ground pork
- 4 ounces boneless, skinless chicken thighs, cut into ¼-inch pieces across the grain
- 4 cups broth (vegetable, chicken, beef, or seafood)
- 1 ounce sliced dried shiitake mushrooms
- 4 ounces medium shrimp, shelled, deveined, and sliced in half lengthwise
- 1 cup bok choy cut into ½-inch pieces
- 4 scallions, both white and green parts, sliced into ¼-inch pieces
- 8 ounces dried vermicelli rice noodles

1. In the wok, heat the oil over high heat until it shimmers.
2. Add the ginger, garlic, pork, and chicken and stir-fry for 3 minutes, until fragrant.
3. Add the broth and dried mushrooms and bring to a boil.
4. Add the shrimp and cook for 1 to 2 minutes, until opaque and curled.
5. Add the bok choy and scallions and simmer for 1 minute, until the pork and chicken are lightly browned.
6. Turn the heat off and add the vermicelli noodles, stirring them into the broth for 2 minutes, until they are al dente.
7. Transfer the softened noodles to your warmed bowls ("crossing the bridge"); distribute the other ingredients among the bowls, pouring the hot broth last, and serve immediately.

Mongolian Beef and Noodles

Prep time: 10 minutes | Cook time: 10 minutes | Serves 4

- 1 pound shaved steak, cut across the grain into 2-inch pieces
- 2 tablespoons Shaoxing cooking wine
- 1 teaspoon cornstarch
- 1 teaspoon Chinese five-spice powder
- 1 tablespoon brown sugar
- 8 ounces dried, or 1 pound fresh lo mein noodles
- 1 tablespoon spicy sesame oil
- 2 tablespoons cooking oil
- 1 tablespoon chopped fresh ginger
- 3 garlic cloves, crushed and chopped
- 1 medium onion, cut into 1-inch pieces
- 1 medium red bell pepper, cut into 1-inch pieces
- 2 tablespoons hoisin sauce
- 4 scallions, both white and green parts, cut into ¼-inch pieces

1. In a large bowl, combine the steak, wine, cornstarch, five-spice powder, and brown sugar and mix well.
2. In a large pot, cook and drain the noodles, then toss them together with sesame oil until well coated and set aside.
3. In the wok, heat the cooking oil over high heat until it shimmers.
4. Add the ginger, garlic, and onion and stir-fry for 1 minute, until fragrant.
5. Add the steak and stir-fry for 1 minute, until lightly browned.
6. Add the bell pepper and stir-fry for 1 minute, until the pepper is fragrant but still crisp.
7. Add the hoisin sauce, scallions, and noodles and stir-fry for 1 minute to mix well. Serve immediately.

Cumin Lamb Noodles (Biang Biang Mein)

Prep time: 10 minutes | Cook time: 5 minutes | Serves 4

- 8 ounces dried or 1 pound fresh pappardelle noodles
- 1 tablespoon spicy sesame oil
- 1 pound ground lamb
- 1 tablespoon ground cumin
- 2 tablespoons Shaoxing cooking wine
- 1 teaspoon cornstarch
- 1 tablespoon red pepper flakes
- 1 tablespoon brown sugar
- 2 tablespoons cooking oil
- 1 tablespoon chopped fresh ginger
- 4 garlic cloves, crushed and chopped
- 1 medium onion, diced into ½-inch pieces
- 4 scallions, both white and green parts, cut into ¼-inch slices
- Fresh cilantro, for garnishing

1. In a large pot, boil the noodles until al dente. Drain, toss with spicy sesame oil, and set aside.
2. In a medium bowl, combine the lamb, cumin, wine, cornstarch, red pepper flakes, and brown sugar. Mix well.
3. In the wok, heat the cooking oil over high heat until it shimmers.
4. Add the ginger, garlic, onion, scallions, and lamb and stir-fry for 3 minutes, until fragrant and browned.
5. Add the noodles and stir-fry for 2 minutes. Garnish with cilantro and serve.

Cantonese Soy and Sesame Panfried Noodles with Scallions And Bean Sprouts

Prep time: 10 minutes | Cook time: 10 minutes | Serves 4

- 1 pound fresh or 8 ounces dried lo mein noodles
- 1 tablespoon toasted sesame oil
- 2 tablespoons light soy sauce
- ¼ cup cooking oil
- 1 tablespoon chopped fresh ginger
- 3 garlic cloves, crushed and chopped
- 4 scallions, both white and green parts, sliced into ¼-inch pieces
- 2 cups fresh bean sprouts

1. In a large pot, boil the noodles until al dente. Drain, toss with toasted sesame oil and soy sauce, and set aside.
2. In the wok, heat the cooking oil over high heat until it shimmers.
3. Add the ginger, garlic, and scallions and stir-fry for 1 minute, until fragrant.
4. Add the noodles and stir-fry for 2 minutes, or until the noodles start to brown and get crispy.
5. Add the bean sprouts, turn off the heat, and toss until the sprouts are mixed in.
6. Serve alone or with another stir-fry dish.

Sambal Pork Noodles

Prep time: 10 minutes | Cook time: 10 minutes | Serves 4

- 1 pound fresh or 8 ounces dry lo mein noodles
- 1 tablespoon spicy sesame oil
- 2 tablespoons cooking oil
- 1 tablespoon chopped fresh ginger
- 4 garlic cloves, crushed and chopped
- 1 pound ground pork
- ¼ cup sambal oelek (see Ingredient tip)
- 1 tablespoon brown sugar
- 1 tablespoon ketchup
- 2 tablespoons dark soy sauce
- 1 tablespoon rice vinegar
- Chopped basil leaves, for garnishing

1. In a large pot, boil the noodles until al dente. Drain, toss with the spicy sesame oil, and set aside.
2. In the wok, heat the cooking oil over high heat until it shimmers.
3. Add the ginger, garlic, and pork and stir-fry for 2 minutes, until fragrant.
4. Add the sambal oelek, brown sugar, ketchup, soy sauce, and vinegar and stir-fry for 2 minutes, until the pork is cooked through.
5. Add the cooked noodles and stir-fry for 1 minute, garnish with basil leaves, and serve.

Guilin Rice Noodles (Mifen)

Prep time: 10 minutes | Cook time: 10 minutes | Serves 4

- 8 cups water
- 8 ounces mifen rice vermicelli
- 1 tablespoon spicy sesame oil
- 8 ounces boneless, skinless chicken thighs, cut across the grain into ¼-inch pieces
- 2 tablespoons Shaoxing cooking wine
- 1 teaspoon cornstarch
- 2 tablespoons Guilin-style chili sauce (such as Lee Yum Kee brand)
- 2 tablespoons cooking oil
- 4 ounces sliced mushrooms
- 4 scallions, both white and green parts, sliced into ¼-inch pieces

1. Bring the water to a boil, then turn off the heat. Soak the dried noodles for 10 minutes, then drain and toss with the sesame oil. Set aside.
2. In a large bowl, combine the chicken, wine, cornstarch, and Guilin sauce. Mix well.
3. In the wok, heat the cooking oil over high heat until it shimmers.
4. Add the chicken and stir-fry for 2 minutes, until lightly browned.
5. Add the mushrooms and scallions and stir-fry for 1 minute, until heated through.
6. Add the noodles and stir-fry for 1 minute to mix well. Serve immediately.

Yangzhou Fried Rice (Yangzhou Chow Fan)

Prep time: 10 minutes | Cook time: 10 minutes | Serves 4 to 6

- 2 tablespoons cooking oil, divided, plus more as needed
- 2 large eggs, lightly beaten
- 8 ounces shrimp, peeled and deveined
- 1 small onion, diced
- ½ cup diced ham
- ½ cup frozen peas (no need to thaw)
- 6 cups cooked white or brown rice (about 2 cups uncooked)
- 1 teaspoon salt
- 2 pinches ground white pepper
- 2 teaspoons light soy sauce
- 3 scallions, both white and green parts, finely chopped

1. In the wok, heat 1 tablespoon of oil over medium-high heat until it shimmers.
2. Pour the eggs into the wok, cook until firm, and use a wok spatula to break them into small pieces. Remove the eggs from the wok and set aside.
3. Add a little more oil to the wok if needed, add the shrimp, and stir-fry until fully cooked. Remove and set aside with the egg.
4. Pour the remaining 1 tablespoon of oil into the wok, and swirl with the wok spatula to coat the bottom surface.
5. Add the onion and diced ham and stir-fry until the onion turns slightly translucent.
6. Add the frozen peas and stir-fry for a few seconds.
7. Add the cooked rice, sprinkle with the salt and white pepper, and drizzle with the soy sauce. Stir-fry for about 1 minute to season and heat the rice.
8. Return the scrambled eggs and shrimp to the wok, then add the chopped scallions, stirring to combine all the ingredients.
9. Serve immediately.

Sichuan Chengdu-Style Fried Rice (Chengdu Chow Fan)

Prep time: 10 minutes | Cook time: 5 minutes | Serves 4

- 2 cups leftover cooked rice, at room temperature
- 1 tablespoon spicy sesame oil
- 1 tablespoon light soy sauce
- 2 tablespoons cooking oil
- 1 tablespoon chopped fresh ginger
- 2 garlic cloves, crushed and chopped
- 8 ounces cured ham, diced into ½-inch pieces
- 3 large eggs, beaten
- 1 medium onion, diced into ½-inch pieces
- 1 medium red bell pepper, diced into ½-inch pieces
- 4 scallions, both white and green parts, sliced into ¼-inch pieces

1. In a large bowl, combine the rice, sesame oil, and soy sauce. Mix well.
2. In the wok, heat the cooking oil over high heat until it shimmers.
3. Add the ginger, garlic, and ham and stir-fry for 1 minute, until fragrant.

4. Add the eggs and stir-fry for about 2 minutes, until the eggs are firm.
5. Add the onion and bell pepper and stir-fry for 1 minute to mix well.
6. Add the rice and scallions and stir-fry for 1 minute to mix. Serve.

Crispy Pork Belly Fried Rice (Siuuk Chow Fan)

Prep time: 10 minutes | Cook time: 10 minutes | Serves 4

- 2 cups leftover cooked rice, at room temperature
- 1 tablespoon toasted sesame oil
- 1 tablespoon light soy sauce
- 4 ounces pork belly, cut into ¼-inch pieces
- 1 tablespoon chopped fresh ginger
- 2 garlic cloves, crushed and chopped
- 1 medium carrot, roll-cut into ½-inch pieces
- 1 cup Brussels sprouts, trimmed and halved
- 3 large eggs, beaten
- 1 medium onion, diced into ½-inch pieces
- 1 medium red bell pepper, diced into ½-inch pieces
- 4 scallions, both white and green parts, sliced into ¼-inch pieces

1. In a bowl, combine the rice, sesame oil, and soy sauce.
2. Heat the wok over medium-high heat and stir-fry the pork belly for 3 minutes, until browned.
3. Add the ginger, garlic, carrot, and Brussels sprouts and stir-fry for 2 minutes, until fragrant. The Brussels sprouts should be bright green.
4. Add the eggs and stir-fry for about 2 minutes, until firm.
5. Add the onion and bell pepper and stir-fry for 1 minute to mix well.
6. Add the rice and scallions and stir-fry for 1 minute to mix well. Serve.

Tea-Smoked Beef and Vegetable Fried Rice

Prep time: 10 minutes | Cook time: 5 minutes | Serves 4

- 2 cups leftover lapsang souchong tea rice
- 1 tablespoon toasted sesame oil
- 1 tablespoon light soy sauce
- 2 tablespoons cooking oil
- 1 tablespoon chopped fresh ginger
- 2 garlic cloves, crushed and chopped
- 8 ounces ground beef
- 2 tablespoons Shaoxing cooking wine
- 3 large eggs, beaten
- 1 medium onion, diced into ½-inch pieces
- 4 scallions, both white and green parts, sliced into ¼-inch pieces

1. In a large bowl, combine the rice, sesame oil, and soy sauce.
2. In the wok, heat the cooking oil over high heat until it shimmers.
3. Add the ginger, garlic, ground beef, and wine and stir-fry for 2 minutes, until browned and fragrant.
4. Add the eggs and stir-fry for 2 minutes, until the eggs are firm.
5. Add the onion and bell pepper and stir-fry for 1 minute to mix well.
6. Add the rice and scallions and stir-fry for 1 minute to mix well. Serve immediately.

Earl Grey Tea Rice with Chinese Sausage and Vegetables

Prep time: 10 minutes | Cook time: 10 minutes | Serves 4

- 2 cups cooked Earl Grey tea rice
- 1 tablespoon toasted sesame oil
- 1 tablespoon light soy sauce
- 2 or 3 lap cheong Chinese sausage links, cut diagonally into ¼-inch-thick ovals
- 1 tablespoon chopped fresh ginger
- 2 garlic cloves, crushed and chopped
- 3 large eggs, beaten
- 1 medium onion, diced into ½-inch pieces
- 4 ounces sliced mushrooms
- 1 medium red bell pepper, cut into ½-inch pieces
- ½ cup frozen corn, thawed
- ½ cup frozen peas, thawed
- 4 scallions, both white and green parts, sliced into ¼-inch pieces

1. In a large bowl, combine the rice, sesame oil, and soy sauce.
2. In the wok over medium heat, combine lap cheong, ginger, and garlic and stir-fry for 2 minutes to render the fat and lightly brown the sausage.
3. Add the eggs and stir-fry for 2 minutes, until firm.
4. Add the onion, mushrooms, and bell pepper and stir-fry for 1 minute.
5. Add the rice, corn, peas, and scallions and stir-fry for 1 minute to mix well. Serve immediately.

Raw Zucchini Noodles with Pesto and Tomatoes

Prep time: 5 minutes | Serves 4

- 3 cups zucchini noodles
- ½ cup good-quality extra-virgin olive oil, divided
- Himalayan pink salt
- Ground black pepper
- 2 cups packed arugula
- ½ cup packed fresh basil leaves
- ¼ cup shredded vegan Parmesan cheese (optional)
- 1 cup grape or cherry tomatoes
- Red pepper flakes

1. Put the zucchini noodles in a shallow baking dish. Pour ¼ cup of the oil over top.
2. Season with salt and black pepper. Toss gently and set aside.
3. In a food processor, combine the arugula, basil, remaining ¼ cup oil, and Parmesan cheese (if using). Process until combined but not totally smooth. Season with salt and black pepper.
4. Transfer the marinated zoodles to a platter. Spoon the pesto over top of the zoodles. Arrange the tomatoes all around and season with red pepper flakes to taste. Enjoy!

Warming Congee with Bitter Greens

Prep time: 5 minutes | Cook time: 45 minutes | Serves 4

- 1 cup sushi rice
- ½ teaspoon sea salt
- 1 (1-inch) piece fresh ginger, peeled and sliced
- 7 cups vegetable broth
- 4 cups chopped, de-stemmed kale, Swiss chard, mustard greens, and|or collard greens

1. Combine the rice, salt, ginger, and broth in a large pot. Bring to a boil over medium heat, then reduce the heat and simmer for 25 minutes, stirring occasionally.
2. Stir in the greens and simmer for an additional 20 minutes, stirring occasionally. Enjoy!

Raw Corn and Vegetable Salad

Prep time: 15 minutes| Serves 4

- 1 seedless cucumber, finely diced
- 2 scallions, sliced
- 1 red bell pepper, seeded and finely diced
- 1½ cups baby kale, chopped
- ½ cup chopped fresh cilantro and|or basil
- 3 cups fresh corn or thawed frozen corn
- ¼ cup finely diced fresh pineapple
- ½ avocado, diced
- 1 (1-inch) piece jalapeño pepper, seeded if desired and finely minced
- Juice of 2 limes

1. Combine all the ingredients in a large bowl and toss well.
2. Let the healing begin!

Spinach and Glass Noodle Salad

Prep time: 10 minutes, plus 15 minutes to rehydrate |Cook time: 10 minutes| Serves 4

- 1 (1½ oz / 40g) bunch glass noodles, soaked in cool water for 15 minutes
- 12 cups (14oz / 400g) lightly packed spinach, cut into 2-inch-long pieces
- 1 tablespoon black vinegar
- 1 teaspoon Chinese light soy sauce
- ½ teaspoon sea salt
- ½ teaspoon granulated sugar
- 3 garlic cloves, minced
- 3 tablespoons canola oil
- 1 tablespoon red Sichuan peppercorns
- 3 dried red facing heaven chili peppers, cut into ¼-inch segments

1. Set up two bowls of cold water. Bring a pot of water to a boil over high heat. Add the noodles and blanch for 4 minutes, then scoop them out of the water (without draining the pot) and transfer them to one of the bowls of cold water to cool. In the same pot, blanch the spinach for 1½ minutes. Drain the spinach and transfer it to the second bowl of cold water to cool.
2. Drain the glass noodles, then use a pair of scissors to cut them into 6-inch-long pieces. Drain the spinach in a colander, then squeeze out as much water as possible.
3. In a medium bowl, combine the noodles, vinegar, soy sauce, salt, and sugar. Put the spinach on top of the noodles and pile the garlic on top.
4. In a wok, heat the oil, Sichuan peppercorns, and chilies over medium heat for 2 minutes, or until the spices are browned and the oil begins to smoke. Discard the chilies and peppercorns and immediately pour the hot oil over the garlic in the bowl.
5. Mix all the ingredients together. Serve as an appetizer or side dish.

Cold Cucumber Herb Soup

Prep time: 5 minutes | Serves 4

- 1 long seedless cucumber with peel, cut into chunks
- 1 garlic clove
- ½ lime with peel, chopped
- 3 scallions with roots, chopped
- 1 cup arugula
- 1 cup fresh dill leaves
- 6 tablespoons fresh cilantro leaves
- 6 tablespoons fresh flat-leaf parsley leaves
- 4 fresh mint leaves
- 4 fresh basil leaves
- ½ cup extra-virgin olive oil
- 2 tablespoons red wine vinegar
- Optional garnishes: generous amounts of hemp seeds, halved grape tomatoes, chopped fresh mint, grated lime zest, red pepper flakes

1. Combine all the ingredients (except garnishes) in a blender. Blend until the mixture is mostly smooth but still has some chunks.
2. Ladle into bowls and pile on the garnishes. Enjoy!

White Bean and Kale Soup

Prep time: 5 minutes | Cook time: 20 minutes | Serves 4

- 1 tablespoon extra-virgin olive oil
- 1 small onion, chopped
- 1 small carrot, peeled and chopped
- 1 celery stalk, chopped
- Sea salt
- Ground black pepper
- 2 garlic cloves, minced
- Leaves from 2 fresh rosemary sprigs, minced
- 2 (15-ounce) cans white beans, rinsed and drained
- 4 cups vegetable broth
- 1 (8-ounce) bunch lacinato (black) kale, thick center ribs removed and discarded, leaves chopped
- Red pepper flakes
- Juice of ½ lemon

1. In a large soup pot, heat the oil over medium heat. Add the onion, carrot, and celery. Season with salt and pepper. Cook, stirring, until the veggies soften a bit, about 5 minutes.
2. Add the garlic, rosemary, beans, and broth. Bring to a boil, then reduce the heat to a simmer.
3. Ladle about half of the contents of the pot into a blender and blend until smooth (see Tip 1). Stir this purée back into the pot.
4. Stir in the kale and red pepper flakes to taste, cover, and cook for 20 minutes.
5. Remove from the heat and stir in the lemon juice.
6. Season to taste with salt and pepper. Enjoy!

Egg Drop Soup

Prep time: 10 minutes | Cook time: 10 minutes | Serves: 4

- 1½ tablespoons cornstarch
- 3 tablespoons water
- 4 cups Basic Chinese Chicken Stock, or store bought
- 1 teaspoon salt
- 2 eggs, lightly beaten
- 1 medium tomato, diced
- Pinch ground white pepper
- 1 scallion, chopped

1. In a small bowl, combine the cornstarch and water.
2. In a wok over medium-high heat, bring the chicken stock to a boil. Add the salt.
3. Stir in the cornstarch-water mixture. Return to a boil.
4. Using a pair of chopsticks, swirl the soup, and at the same time slowly pour the beaten eggs into the soup. Swirl faster for a thinner, silky consistency; or slower for a thicker, chunky egg consistency.
5. Add the tomato and pepper, stir, and simmer for 1 minute.
6. Garnish with the scallion, and serve.

Lotus Root with Pork Ribs Soup

Prep time: 10 minutes | Cook time: 4 Hours | Serves: 6-8

- 1 pound pork ribs, cut into 1-inch pieces
- 1 pound lotus root, peeled and cut into ¼-inch-thick rounds
- ½ teaspoon peppercorns
- ½ cup dried red dates (optional)
- 12 cups water
- 2 tablespoons soy sauce
- 1 teaspoon salt
- ¼ cup dried goji berries

1. Place the pork ribs, lotus root, peppercorns, red dates (if using), and water in a wok.
2. Simmer over low heat for at least 4 hours, and up to 6 hours.
3. Turn off the heat and add the soy sauce, salt, and goji berries.
4. Allow the soup to sit for about 15 minutes for the goji berries to reconstitute, then serve.

Hot and Sour Soup

Prep time: 10 minutes | Cook time: 10 minutes | Serves: 6-8

- 6 cups Basic Chinese Chicken Stock, or store bought
- 4 tablespoons water
- 2 tablespoons cornstarch
- 2 tablespoons soy sauce
- 1 teaspoon dark soy sauce
- ¼ cup rice vinegar or apple cider vinegar
- 2 teaspoons sesame oil
- 2 teaspoons brown sugar
- 2 pinches ground white pepper
- 2 teaspoons Sichuan chili oil
- ½ cup diced firm tofu
- 4 large shiitake mushrooms, soaked then cut into thin strips
- ½ cup dried wood ear mushrooms, soaked and cut into thin strips
- ¼ cup sliced bamboo shoots
- 2 eggs, lightly beaten

1. In a wok over medium-high heat, bring the chicken stock to a boil.
2. Combine the water and cornstarch in a small bowl and set it aside.
3. Add the soy sauce, dark soy sauce, vinegar, sesame oil, brown sugar, white pepper, and chili oil.
4. Add the tofu, shiitake mushrooms, wood ear mushrooms, and bamboo shoots. Bring to a boil.
5. While stirring, slowly add the cornstarch mixture. Return to a boil.
6. Use chopsticks to stir the soup while slowly pouring the beaten eggs into the soup. The faster you swirl and the faster you pour, the silkier the egg. Swirl and pour slowly for a chunkier egg texture.

Watercress and Pork Soup

Prep time: 10 minutes | Cook time: 4 Hours | Serves: 6-8

- 12 cups water, divided
- ½ pound pork ribs or pork shoulder, cut into 1-inch pieces
- 6 to 10 dried red dates
- ¼ cup dried goji berries
- 1 pound watercress
- 1 tablespoon salt
- 3 pinches ground white pepper

1. In a wok, bring 2 cups of water to a boil. Blanch the pork for about 5 minutes. Rinse the pork and the wok, and set the pork aside.
2. In the wok, bring the remaining 10 cups of water to a boil.
3. Return the pork to the wok. Reduce the heat to low and simmer, partially covered, for 3½ hours.
4. Add the red dates, goji berries, watercress, salt, and pepper. Simmer for 10 more minutes, and serve.

Chicken and Sweet Corn Soup

Prep time: 10 minutes | Cook time: 10 minutes | Serves: 6-8

- 2 (14.75-ounce) cans cream-style sweet corn
- 8 cups Basic Chinese Chicken Stock or store bought
- 2 cups cooked shredded chicken
- 1 teaspoon salt
- 1 teaspoon sesame oil
- 3 teaspoons cornstarch mixed with 2 tablespoons water (optional)
- 2 eggs, lightly beaten
- 1 scallion, chopped

1. In a wok over high heat, add the corn to the chicken stock and bring to a boil.
2. Add the shredded chicken, salt, and sesame oil. Return to a boil.
3. Stir in the cornstarch mixture (if using) to thicken the soup. Return to a boil.
4. Use chopsticks to stir the soup and while stirring, pour the beaten eggs into the soup. The faster you swirl and the faster you pour, the silkier the egg. Swirl and pour slowly for a chunkier egg texture.
5. Garnish with the chopped scallion just before serving.

Sweet Peanut Soup

Prep time: 5 Minutes, Plus 10 To 26 Hours Inactive | Cook time: 2 Hours | Serves: 4

- ½ pound raw peanuts, shelled and skinned
- 1 tablespoon baking soda
- 8 cups water, plus more for soaking
- 4 tablespoons sugar

1. Soak the peanuts in a bowl of water overnight.
2. Rinse the peanuts, sprinkle them with the baking soda, then cover in fresh water to soak for 1 to 2 more hours.
3. Thoroughly rinse the peanuts.
4. In a wok over high heat, bring the 8 cups of water to a boil.
5. Add the peanuts to the boiling water, reduce the heat to low, and simmer, partially covered, for 2 hours.
6. Add the sugar in increments until the soup reaches your desired sweetness.
7. Serve the soup at room temperature, hot, or cold, with an almond or butter cookie, if desired.

Cabbage and Pork Meatball Soup

Prep time: 15 Minutes, Plus 15 Minutes To Marinate | Cook time: 35 minutes | Serves: 8-10

FOR THE PORK MEATBALLS

½ pound ground pork
¼ pound minced shrimp (4 to 6 large shrimp)
¼ cup finely diced water chestnuts
1 teaspoon soy sauce
½ teaspoon sugar
½ teaspoon salt
Pinch ground white pepper
1½ tablespoons cornstarch
FOR THE SOUP
10 cups Basic Chinese Chicken Stock, or store bought
½ head napa cabbage, cut into 1-inch pieces
1 carrot, sliced
2 teaspoons salt
2 teaspoons sesame oil
2 teaspoons soy sauce

TO MAKE THE MEATBALLS

1. In a bowl, mix the ground pork, shrimp, water chestnuts, soy sauce, sugar, salt, pepper, and cornstarch. Set aside to marinate for about 15 minutes.

TO MAKE THE SOUP

1. In a wok over high heat, bring the chicken stock to a boil.
2. Add the cabbage and carrot, and simmer for about 30 minutes.
3. Roll about 1 heaping tablespoon of pork mixture into a ball and continue until all the pork mixture is used. Carefully drop the meatballs into the boiling soup one at a time. Avoid stirring. As the meatballs cook, they will rise to the top. They will take about 3 minutes to cook through.
4. Add the salt, sesame oil, and soy sauce just before turning off the heat.

Chinese Mushroom Soup

Prep time: 10 minutes | Cook time: 25 minutes | Serves: 6

*   1 tablespoon olive oil
*   ½ onion, sliced
*   2 garlic cloves, minced
*   1 carrot, cut into thin slices
*   4 or 5 large shiitake mushrooms, cut into thin slices
*   5 or 6 white or brown button mushrooms, cut into thin slices
*   1 small bunch enoki mushrooms, roots removed
*   8 cups vegetable stock
*   ¼ cup dried goji berries
*   2 teaspoons sesame oil
*   1 tablespoon soy sauce
*   1 teaspoon salt

1. In a wok over medium heat, heat the olive oil.
2. Sauté the onion and garlic until the onion turns slightly translucent.
3. Add the carrot, shiitake mushrooms, button mushrooms, and enoki mushrooms. Sauté for about 1 minute.
4. Pour in the vegetable stock and bring to a boil.
5. Add the goji berries, sesame oil, soy sauce, and salt.
6. Simmer over low heat for about 20 minutes before serving.

Wonton Soup

Prep time: 20 minutes | Cook time: 10 minutes | Serves: 6-8

FOR THE WONTONS

*   ¼ pound ground pork
*   ¼ pound shrimp, peeled, deveined, and roughly chopped
*   1 teaspoon cornstarch
*   1 teaspoon sesame oil
*   1 teaspoon soy sauce
*   ½ teaspoon salt
*   Pinch ground white pepper
*   20 to 25 square wonton wrappers
*   FOR THE SOUP
*   8 cups Basic Chinese Chicken Stock, or store bought
*   2 tablespoons low-sodium soy sauce
*   2 teaspoons sesame oil
*   3 pinches ground white pepper
*   1 scallion, chopped

TO MAKE THE WONTONS

1. In a bowl, mix together the pork, shrimp, cornstarch, sesame oil, soy sauce, salt, and pepper.
2. Place about 1 teaspoon of pork mixture in the center of a wonton wrapper.
3. Dampen your finger with water and run it along the edge of the wonton to help seal it, then fold the wonton in half into a triangle. Gently press the edges to seal.
4. Fold the bottom two corners (just outside the meat filling) toward each other, and press those corners together to seal them. Set the wontons aside.

TO MAKE THE SOUP

1. Bring the chicken stock to a boil in a wok over high heat. Add the soy sauce

Chicken Stock with Ginger

Prep time: 15 minutes | Cook time: 1 hour 45 minutes | Makes 12 cups

- 5 pounds chicken parts
- 16 cups water, divided, plus more as needed
- 1 (2-inch) piece fresh ginger, thinly sliced
- 1 teaspoon salt

1. Place the chicken in the Instant Pot and pour in 4 cups of water. Select Sauté and bring the water to a boil. Parboil for 5 minutes, or until the water starts to foam. Select Cancel.
2. In a large colander in the sink, drain the chicken and rinse it to remove any impurities. Rinse and dry the liner before returning it to the base.
3. Return the chicken to the Instant Pot and pour in the remaining 12 cups of water, or as needed to reach the maximum fill line. Add the ginger and salt.
4. Lock the lid. Program to pressure cook using the Soup function for 60 minutes on high pressure.
5. When the timer sounds, let the pressure release naturally for 30 minutes, then quick release any remaining pressure.
6. Carefully remove the lid. Remove the chicken (reserve the meat for other uses) and strain the stock through a fine-mesh sieve into a large pot. Or, if using the stock later, transfer to Mason jars or freezer-safe containers and cool in an ice bath. Refrigerate for up to 1 week, or freeze for up to 2 months.

Chicken and Pork Stock

Prep time: 15 minutes | Cook time: 1 hour 45 minutes | Makes 12 cups

- 2 pounds bone-in skin-on chicken breasts or drumsticks
- 1 pound lean pork, cut into 4 pieces
- 1 pound pork bones
- 16 cups water, divided, plus more as needed
- 1 (1-inch) piece fresh ginger, thinly sliced
- 2 teaspoons salt

1. In the Instant Pot, combine the chicken, pork, and pork bones, then pour in 4 cups of water. Select Sauté and bring to a boil. Parboil for 10 minutes, or until foam starts to form. Select Cancel.
2. In a large colander in the sink, drain the chicken, pork, and bones and rinse them to remove any impurities. Rinse and dry the pot before returning it to the base.
3. Return the chicken, pork, and pork bones to the Instant Pot and add the ginger and salt. Pour in the remaining 12 cups of water, or as needed to reach the maximum fill line.
4. Lock the lid. Program to pressure cook using the Soup function for 60 minutes on high pressure.
5. When the timer sounds, let the pressure release naturally for 30 minutes, then quick release any remaining pressure.
6. Carefully remove the lid. Remove the chicken, pork, and bones (reserve the meat for other uses) and strain the stock through a fine-mesh sieve into a large pot. Or, if using the stock later, transfer to Mason jars or freezer-safe containers and cool in an ice bath. Refrigerate for up to 1 week, or freeze for up to 2 months.

Bok Choy, Pork, and Vermicelli Soup

Prep time: 15 minutes | Cook time: 15 minutes | Serves 6

- 1 bundle mung bean rice vermicelli
- 8 ounces baby bok choy
- 4 ounces lean pork, thinly sliced or julienned
- 1 teaspoon rice wine
- ¼ teaspoon salt
- Ground white pepper
- 1 teaspoon cornstarch
- 1 teaspoon neutral oil
- 1 (½-inch) piece fresh ginger, thinly sliced
- 4 cups Chicken Stock with Ginger or Chicken and Pork Stock
- 2 carrots, cut into ¼-inch rounds
- 2 tablespoons chopped scallion, white and green parts

1. In a medium bowl, soak the mung bean vermicelli in cold water for 5 minutes. Drain and use scissors to cut the vermicelli in half. Set aside.
2. If the baby bok choy are 2 to 3 inches long, halve them lengthwise; otherwise chop them crosswise into 1-inch pieces. Set aside.
3. In a small bowl, mix the pork, wine, salt, and ¼ teaspoon of pepper. Add the cornstarch and mix again. Set aside.
4. On the Instant Pot, select Sauté to preheat the pot. Once hot, pour in the oil and add the ginger. Stir-fry for 1 minute until fragrant. Add the pork mixture and stir-fry for about 2 minutes until no longer pink.
5. Pour in the stock to deglaze the pot, scraping up any browned bits from the bottom. Add the carrots, bok choy, and vermicelli.
6. Lock the lid. Program to pressure cook for 1 minute on high pressure.
7. When the timer sounds, let the pressure release naturally for 5 minutes, then quick release the remaining pressure.
8. Serve with a sprinkle of scallion and a pinch of pepper.

Westlake Soup (Minced Beef and Egg Soup)

Prep time: 15 minutes | Cook time: 35 minutes | Serves 4

- 4 ounces beef
- 1 teaspoon light soy sauce
- 1 teaspoon neutral oil
- 4 ounces mushrooms (any kind), chopped
- 6 ounces silken or soft tofu, drained and cut into ½-inch cubes
- ¼ teaspoon salt
- Ground white pepper
- 4 cups Chicken Stock with Ginger
- 3 tablespoons water
- 3 tablespoons cornstarch
- 4 large egg whites, lightly beaten, or 2 large eggs
- 1 cup chopped fresh cilantro, plus more for serving

1. To mince the beef, using a cleaver or large chef's knife, cut the beef into strips and then into small cubes before chopping until the beef is minced. Transfer to a small bowl and stir in the soy sauce. Set aside.
2. On the Instant Pot, select Sauté to preheat the pot. Once hot, pour in the oil and add the mushrooms. Stir-fry for 3 to 4 minutes until the mushrooms are soft.
3. Add the beef, tofu, salt, and ⅛ teaspoon of pepper and pour in the stock.
4. Lock the lid. Program to pressure cook using the Soup function for 5 minutes on high pressure.
5. In a small bowl, whisk the water and cornstarch. Set aside.
6. When the timer sounds, let the pressure release naturally for 10 minutes, then quick release the remaining pressure. Carefully remove the lid.
7. Select Sauté. Whisk the cornstarch slurry, then stir it into the soup. Cook for about 2 minutes, or until the soup begins to bubble and thicken.
8. Slowly drizzle in the egg whites. Wait 15 seconds, then stir gently in one direction. Add the cilantro.
9. Serve the soup with a pinch of pepper and more cilantro, as desired.

Hot and Sour Tofu and Vegetable Soup

Prep time: 15 minutes | Cook time: 30 minutes | Serves 4

- 3 tablespoons cornstarch
- 2 tablespoons rice vinegar or black vinegar
- 1 tablespoon light soy sauce
- 1 teaspoon neutral oil
- 8 ounces mushrooms (any type), chopped
- ¼ teaspoon salt
- 4 cups vegetable broth
- 14 ounces soft or silken tofu, cut into ½-inch cubes
- 2 large carrots, julienned (about 1 cup)
- ½ (8-ounce) can bamboo shoots, julienned
- Ground white pepper or freshly ground black pepper
- 2 large eggs, lightly beaten
- 1 teaspoon chili oil (optional)
- ¼ cup chopped scallion, white and green parts, or fresh cilantro

1. In a small bowl, whisk the cornstarch, vinegar, and soy sauce. Set aside.
2. On the Instant Pot, select Sauté to preheat the pot. Once hot, pour in the oil and add the mushrooms and salt. Stir-fry for about 2 minutes until soft.
3. Pour in the broth and add the tofu, carrots, bamboo shoots, and ½ teaspoon of pepper.
4. Lock the lid. Program to pressure cook using the Soup function for 1 minute on high pressure.
5. When the timer sounds, quick release the pressure. Carefully remove the lid.
6. Select Sauté. Whisk the cornstarch slurry, then stir it into the soup. Cook until the soup bubbles, then drizzle in the eggs in a circular motion. Wait 15 seconds, add the chili oil (if using; alternatively add chili oil to taste in each bowl after serving), then stir the soup gently. Select Cancel.
7. Serve garnished with a sprinkle of chopped scallion and a light sprinkle of pepper.

Scallop, Shrimp, and Crab Soup

Prep time: 15 minutes | Cook time: 35 minutes| Serves 6

- 6 ounces frozen bay scallops, thawed
- 6 ounces frozen bay shrimp, thawed
- 3 carrots, chopped
- 1½ cups frozen corn kernels
- 8 ounces soft or silken tofu, diced small
- 2 garlic cloves, minced
- ½ teaspoon salt
- ¼ teaspoon ground white pepper
- 4 cups water, plus 3 tablespoons, divided
- 3 tablespoons cornstarch
- 1 (6-ounce) can crabmeat, drained
- 6 ounces snow peas or snap peas, halved, fibrous end and string removed
- 2 large eggs, lightly beaten
- 2 scallions, white and green parts, chopped

1. In a medium bowl, combine the scallops with enough water to cover and swish to release any sand. Repeat, changing the water as needed, until the scallops are clean and free of sand. Set aside. Peel the shrimp, if needed.
2. In the Instant Pot, combine the carrots, corn kernels, tofu, and garlic. Add the scallops, shrimp, salt, ¼ teaspoon of pepper, and 4 cups of water.
3. Lock the lid. Program to pressure cook using the Soup function for 2 minutes on high pressure.
4. In a small bowl, whisk the cornstarch and remaining 3 tablespoons of water. Set aside.
5. When the timer sounds, let the pressure release naturally for 5 minutes, then quick release the remaining pressure. Carefully remove the lid.
6. Select Sauté and add the crabmeat and snow peas. Whisk the cornstarch slurry, then add it to the soup and stir to combine. Cook for about 4 minutes until the soup begins to bubble and thicken.
7. Slowly drizzle in the eggs in a circular motion. Wait 15 seconds, then stir gently.
8. Serve with a pinch of pepper and chopped scallions as garnish.

Mom'S Beef Meatball, Potato, and Carrot Soup

Prep time: 25 minutes | Cook time: 35 minutes| Serves 6

- 8 ounces lean beef (any tender cut) or lean ground beef
- 1 teaspoon cornstarch
- Ground white pepper
- 4 cups Chicken Stock with Ginger or water
- 4 carrots, chopped (about 1½ cups)
- 2 large potatoes, peeled and chopped (about 1½ cups)
- 1 (½-inch) piece fresh ginger, minced
- 1 garlic clove, chopped
- ½ teaspoon salt
- ¼ cup chopped scallion, white and green parts

1. If mincing the beef, using a cleaver or a large chef's knife, cut the beef into strips, then into small cubes, and then mince it. Transfer the beef to a medium bowl and stir in the cornstarch and ⅛ teaspoon of pepper. Divide the meat mixture into 8 equal portions and shape each into a meatball.
2. In the Instant Pot, combine the stock, carrots, potatoes, ginger, garlic, and salt. Place the meatballs on top.
3. Lock the lid. Program to pressure cook using the Soup function for 5 minutes on high pressure.
4. When the timer sounds, let the pressure release naturally for 10 minutes, then quick release the remaining pressure.
5. Serve with a sprinkle of chopped scallion and a pinch of pepper.

Red Bean and Tapioca Tong Sui

Prep time: 5 minutes | Cook time:1 hour 25 minutes| Serves 6

- 6 cups water
- 1 cup dried adzuki beans, rinsed and picked over for debris
- 1 teaspoon dried Valencia orange peel
- ½ cup (3 to 4 ounces) rock sugar
- ⅓ cup small tapioca pearls

1. Pour the water into the Instant Pot and add the beans and Valencia peel.
2. Lock the lid. Program to pressure cook for 45 minutes on high pressure.
3. When the timer sounds, let the pressure release naturally for 15 minutes.
4. Carefully remove the lid. Select Sauté and adjust the heat to low. Add the rock sugar and tapioca pearls. Cook for about 20 minutes, stirring every 5 minutes, or until the tapioca pearls are translucent and no longer white.
5. Select Cancel, then select Keep Warm until ready to serve.

Chapter 11
Dumplings, Egg Rolls, And Dim Sum Favorites

Classic Egg Rolls

Prep time: 10 minutes | Cook time: 15-29 minutes | Serves 8-10

FOR THE MARINADE

- 2 tablespoons soy sauce
- 2 tablespoons oyster sauce
- 1 teaspoon rice vinegar
- 3 cloves garlic, minced
- 2 teaspoons fresh ginger, minced
- ½ teaspoon brown sugar

FOR THE EGG ROLLS

- 1 pound ground pork
- 1 tablespoon cornstarch
- 2 tablespoons vegetable oil
- 2 cups cabbage, shredded
- 1 medium carrot, peeled and shredded
- Salt and pepper
- 1 package egg roll wrappers
- Peanut oil for deep frying

1. Combine the ingredients for the marinade in a bowl, blending well.
2. Add the ground pork and cornstarch and combine. It's best to use your hands, clean or gloved, to do this.
3. Let the mixture marinade for about 5 minutes.
4. In a wok, heat the vegetable oil over medium heat. Stir-fry the pork until it is no longer pink.
5. Add the cabbage and carrots, and cook until heated through (about 2 minutes).
6. Season with salt and pepper as desired, and remove from the heat.
7. Place one wrapper at a time on a clean surface or tray, in a diamond shape.
8. Add about ¼ or ⅓ cup of the pork filling close to the tip of the diamond at the bottom, closest to you. Do not put too much filling or the wrapper will break while frying.
9. Fold the bottom tip of the wrapper over the filling. Roll tightly once.
10. Fold the left and right corners inward, and continue rolling up to the top corner.
11. Moisten the top corner with a little water or a paste of water and cornstarch to seal the roll.
12. Repeat until all the filling or wrappers are used up.Prepare the peanut oil by heating it in a wok over medium-high heat. The oil is ready when wooden chopsticks immersed in the oil release tiny bubbles.
13. Working in batches, fry the rolls until they are golden brown. For more efficient heating and to get crisp rolls, do not overcrowd the rolls in the oil.
14. Use a spider strainer or tongs to lift the rolls out of the oil, and place them in a dish lined with paper towels.
15. Serve hot.

Vegetable Spring Rolls

Prep time: 45 minutes | Cook time: 30 minutes | Serves 8

- 1 ½ cups bean sprouts
- 8 shiitake mushrooms
- 1 tablespoon sesame oil
- 3 green onions, trimmed and diced
- 3 cloves, garlic, minced
- 1 teaspoon ginger, freshly grated
- 2 medium carrots, shredded
- 2 ½ cups green cabbage, shredded
- 8 ounces canned bamboo shoots, drained and thinly sliced
- 2 tablespoons low-sodium soya sauce
- 2 tablespoons peanut (or any other preferred) oil
- 50 spring roll wrappers, thawed
- 1 egg, beaten with 2 tablespoons of water
- Oil for frying

1. Wash and drain the bean sprouts. Set them aside.
2. Wash and pat the mushrooms dry. Julienne them very finely.
3. Heat 1 tablespoon of sesame oil in a skillet or wok over medium-high heat. Add the green onions, garlic, and ginger. Stir-fry for about 1 minute.
4. Add the remaining vegetables. Sauté until tender, about 3-4 minutes.
5. Add the soya sauce and peanut oil. Stir to combine well. Cook for 1 more minute and remove it from the heat.
6. Place the filling in a strainer to remove most of the cooking liquids. Place the filling in a bowl.
7. Open your package of spring rolls and place all but one wrapper under a clean, damp, dish cloth to ensure the wrappers do not dry out.
8. Set your wrapper on flat surface with one corner pointed at you.
9. Place a generous tablespoon of filling on the bottom of the wrapper, about two inches above the corner point.
10. Fold the bottom part of the wrapper over the filling, and then fold the sides over the filling, so you have what almost looks like an envelope with a long flap.
11. Roll the spring roll away from you until you get about two inches from the top, brush the edges at the top with your egg wash, complete roll and repeat.
12. Keep finished rolls under clean, damp, dish cloth as well.
13. Once you have all of your rolls set, line a plate with paper towels.

Pork Spring Rolls

Prep time: 30 minutes plus 20 minutes marinating time |
Cook time: 30 minutes | Serves 5

- 2 pounds ground pork
- For marinade
- 2 tablespoons cornstarch
- 2 tablespoons rice wine vinegar
- 2 tablespoons rice wine
- 1 teaspoon salt
- 1 teaspoon ground black pepper

FOR DIPPING SAUCE

- 2 tablespoons water
- 2 ½ teaspoons sugar
- 4 tablespoons hot sauce
- 6 tablespoons soy sauce
- 2 tablespoons rice vinegar
- 2 teaspoons rice wine

FOR FILLING

- 4 tablespoons vegetable oil, divided
- 10 cups cabbage, shredded
- 2 large carrots, shredded
- 3 cloves garlic, minced
- 1 teaspoon fresh ginger, peeled and grated
- 1 8-ounce can bamboo shoots, drained, squeezed, and shredded
- 10 dried shiitake mushrooms, rehydrated in boiling water, squeezed, and minced
- 1 cup green onion, chopped
- 2 tablespoons cornstarch
- 1 teaspoon sugar
- 4 tablespoons soy sauce
- 2 teaspoons sesame oil
- 2 tablespoons rice wine
- 50 spring roll wrappers
- Oil for frying

FOR THE PORK

1. In a large bowl, combine the ingredients for the marinade. Add the pork and mix well. Allow the mixture to marinate for 15-20 minutes.
2. For the dipping sauce
3. In another bowl, whisk together the ingredients for the dipping sauce. Set it aside to allow the flavors to meld.

FOR THE FILLING

1. Heat 2 tablespoons of oil in a wok over medium heat. Blanch the cabbage in the oil quickly, for about 2 minutes. Adjust the heat, if needed, to avoid scorching. Using a slotted spoon, remove the cabbage from the oil and set it aside to cool on a plate.
2. Using whatever oil is left in the wok (you may add another tablespoon, if needed), cook the carrots the same way. Remove the carrots from the oil using a slotted spoon and set them aside to cool.
3. Add the remaining oil to the wok and heat. Add the marinated pork and cook until the pork is browned and all the liquid is reduced.

4. Add the garlic and ginger and cook about 2-3 minutes longer. Do not burn the garlic.
5. Add the bamboo and mushrooms and heat through, about 3-5 minutes.
6. Remove the wok from the heat and set it aside to cool.
7. When the pork mixture has cooled down, add the cabbage and carrots, together with the mushrooms, green onion, cornstarch, sugar, soy sauce, sesame oil, and rice wine. Mix thoroughly.

TO MAKE THE ROLLS

8. Place a wrapper on a clean surface. Position it so that it is diamond-shaped.
9. Place about ¼-⅓ cup of filling on the wrapper, about 1 ½ to 2 inches from the bottom corner.
10. Fold the bottom corner over the filling and roll snugly upwards once.
11. Fold in right and left corners and continue rolling up to top corner.
12. Moisten the top corner with water to help seal the roll. You may also use a paste of water and cornstarch as an adhesive to make it stick better.
13. Repeat until the filling is used up. You should be able to make about 50 rolls.
14. Heat the cooking or peanut oil in a wok or frying pan, about 2 inches deep, over medium heat.
15. Fry the rolls until they are golden brown. For efficient frying and crisp rolls, do not fry too many rolls at once; fry them in several batches.
16. Use a spider strainer to fish out the finished rolls, and place them on a dish lined with paper towels.
17. Serve while hot with the dipping sauce. The rolls may also be halved diagonally before serving.
18. Fill a heavy pot halfway up with oil for frying. Warm the oil on medium heat until it reaches 350°F. You can also use a wok or a deep fryer. Deep fry spring rolls until they are golden, about 1-2 minutes on each side.
14. Place spring rolls on a plate lined with paper towels to absorb any excess oil before serving.
15. Serve with your favorite dipping sauce.

Shrimp Rice Paper Rolls

Prep time: 35 minutes | Cook time: 15 minutes| Serves 4

- 4 round rice paper sheets
- Lettuce or cabbage leaves, for lining bowls
- 4 tablespoons water, divided, plus 1½ cups
- 8 ounces jumbo (26 count) shrimp, peeled and deveined
- 2 tablespoons light soy sauce
- 1 teaspoon sugar
- ½ teaspoon chicken bouillon
- 1 tablespoon fried shallot or onion (optional)
- 1 tablespoon chopped scallion, white and green parts (optional)

1. Fill a large bowl with water. One at a time, drop the rice paper sheets into the water and soak for 5 minutes. Set aside while preparing the remaining ingredients.
2. Line two pressure-safe bowls with lettuce leaves and add 1 tablespoon of water to each bowl. Set aside.
3. Place a sheet of rice paper on a work surface and arrange 3 shrimp on the bottom third of the sheet. Roll up the sheet halfway, tuck in the sides, and roll it the rest of the way. Place the roll in a prepared bowl and repeat to make one more shrimp roll.
4. Pour 1 cup of water into the Instant Pot and place a trivet inside. Place the filled bowl on the trivet.
5. Lock the lid. Program to pressure cook for 2 minutes on high pressure.
6. While the first two rolls steam, roll the remaining shrimp and rice sheets (repeat step 3) and place them in the second prepared bowl.
7. When the timer sounds, quick release the pressure and carefully remove the lid and bowl.
8. Pour the remaining ½ cup of water into the pot and repeat the process (steps 4 and 5) for steaming the second batch.
9. In a small bowl, stir together the soy sauce, remaining 2 tablespoons of water, sugar, and chicken bouillon. Drizzle each steamed roll with 1 teaspoon of sauce and garnish with fried shallot (if using) and scallion (if using). Cut the rolls into thirds and serve with any extra sauce on the side.

Pork and Shrimp Shumai

Prep time: 25 minutes | Cook time: 15 minutes| Makes 15 to 25 dumplings

- ½ pound shrimp, peeled and deveined
- ½ pound ground pork
- 3 tablespoons sesame oil
- 1 tablespoon cornstarch
- 1 tablespoon soy sauce
- 1 teaspoon grated ginger
- ½ teaspoon salt
- 2 pinches ground white pepper
- 2 teaspoons Shaoxing wine
- 20 to 25 round wonton wrappers
- ½ carrot, finely minced

1. Mince the shrimp by flattening each piece with the side of a knife, then roughly chopping each one.
2. Mix together the shrimp and the ground pork.
3. Add the sesame oil, cornstarch, soy sauce, ginger, salt, pepper, and Shaoxing wine to the shrimp and pork. Combine thoroughly.
4. Make an "O" with your thumb and index finger. Place one wonton wrapper on the "O" and gently press it down to create a small cup.
5. Using a teaspoon, fill the wonton cup to the top with some of the pork and shrimp mixture. Use the back of the teaspoon to press the filling into the cup.
6. Line a bamboo steamer with parchment paper liners or napa cabbage leaves. Arrange the shumai on top of the liners or leaves. Top each shumai with a bit of minced carrot.
7. Steam for 10 minutes or until the meat is cooked through.

Fried Wontons

Prep time: 1 ½ hours | Cook time: 20 minutes | Serves 5

- 1 pack (about 50 pieces) wonton wrappers
- Oil for frying
- For the filling
- 1 pound ground pork
- 2 tablespoons scallions, finely chopped
- 1 teaspoon sesame oil
- 1 tablespoon soy sauce
- 1 tablespoon rice wine
- ½ teaspoon sugar
- 1 tablespoon peanut oil
- ⅛ teaspoon ground white pepper

- For the dipping sauce
- 1 tablespoon water
- 1 tablespoon sugar
- 1 ½ tablespoons light soy sauce
- 1 teaspoon Worcestershire sauce
- ½ teaspoon rice vinegar
- 1 teaspoon toasted sesame seeds

FOR THE FILLING

1. Combine all the ingredients for the filling and mix thoroughly, with your hands or a food processor, until the mixture is paste-like in consistency.

TO MAKE THE WONTONS

2. Line a baking sheet or tray with parchment paper.
3. Place a wrapper on a plate or clean surface, and put about a teaspoon of filling on the center.
4. Moisten the wrapper with a dab of water around the filling. This will help the sides of the wrapper to stick together.
5. Fold into either a rectangle or a triangle, pressing the edges together to seal. For rectangles, bring bottom corners together until they overlap, moisten with water, and press to seal. For triangles, bring the side corners together until they overlap and seal. Repeat until the filling is used up. Makes about 40-50 wontons.
6. Arrange the wontons on the lined baking sheet, leaving space to prevent sticking.
7. To store them, cover with plastic wrap and freeze. They keep for 2 months when frozen.

FOR DIPPING SAUCE

8. Prepare the sauce before frying the wontons, so the flavors can meld while the sauce is left standing.
9. Simply whisk the sauce ingredients together in a bowl.

TO FRY

10. Heat enough oil for frying in a wok or pan over medium heat. The oil should be 2 to 3 inches deep.
11. Fry the wontons in batches, turning over if needed, or keeping them submerged for even frying.
12. Let them drain on paper towels.
13. Serve with the dipping sauce.

Steamed Vegetable Dumplings

Prep time: 25 minutes | Cook time: 15 minutes| Makes 15 to 20 dumplings

FOR THE DUMPLINGS

- 2 teaspoons olive oil
- 4 cups shredded cabbage
- 1 carrot, shredded
- 2 scallions, chopped
- 5 to 8 garlic chives, cut into 1-inch pieces
- 1-inch piece of ginger, peeled and minced
- 1 tablespoon water
- 2 teaspoons sesame oil, plus 2 teaspoons for brushing
- Salt
- Pepper
- 15 to 20 round wonton wrappers

FOR THE DIPPING SAUCE

- 2 tablespoons soy sauce
- 2 teaspoons sesame oil
- 2 teaspoons rice vinegar
- 1 teaspoon chili oil
- 1-inch piece of ginger, peeled and finely minced

1. In a wok over medium heat, heat the olive oil.
2. Add the cabbage, carrot, scallions, garlic chives, and ginger to the wok. Stir-fry for about 1 minute.
3. Add the water to help steam the vegetables. Stir-fry until most of the water has evaporated. Drizzle 2 teaspoons of sesame oil over the vegetables. Season with salt and pepper, and toss. Remove from the heat and set it aside to cool.
4. Place about 1 teaspoon of vegetable mixture in the middle of a wonton wrapper.
5. Dampen the edges of the wonton wrapper with a little water, fold the wrapper in half so that it forms a triangle, and gently press down to seal the edges.
6. Brush the dumplings with a light coating of sesame oil.
7. Line a bamboo steamer with parchment paper liners or napa cabbage leaves. Arrange the dumplings on top and steam for 8 minutes, or until the wonton wrappers look slightly translucent.
8. While the dumplings are steaming, make the dipping sauce. Combine the soy sauce, sesame oil, rice vinegar, chili oil, and ginger in a small bowl.
9. Serve the dumplings with the dipping sauce.

Shrimp Dumplings

Prep time: 35 minutes | Cook time: 15 minutes| Makes 15 to 20 dumplings

FOR THE FILLING

- 1 pound peeled and deveined shrimp, roughly chopped
- ¼ cup diced water chestnuts
- 1½ tablespoons sesame oil
- 2 teaspoons soy sauce
- 2 tablespoons cornstarch
- 2 tablespoons finely chopped fresh cilantro (optional)

FOR THE WRAPPERS

- 1¼ cups wheat starch
- 2 tablespoons tapioca flour
- 1¼ cups boiling water
- 1 teaspoon peanut oil

TO MAKE THE FILLING

1. In a large bowl, combine the shrimp, water chestnuts, sesame oil, soy sauce, and cornstarch. Add the cilantro (if using). Mix well.
2. Marinate the mixture in the refrigerator for at least 30 minutes.

TO MAKE THE WRAPPERS

3. In a large bowl, combine the wheat starch and tapioca flour.
4. Slowly pour the boiling water into the flour mixture while stirring, until it starts to form a ball of dough.
5. Cover the bowl with a damp towel and allow the dough to cool down slightly before handling.
6. Cover your palms, a small rolling pin, and a cutting board with a bit of peanut oil to prevent the dough from sticking.
7. Knead the dough for 2 to 3 minutes.
8. Take about a teaspoon of dough and gently roll it into a ball.
9. Roll the dough out into a small pancake, about 3 inches in diameter.

TO MAKE THE DUMPLINGS

10. Set up a bamboo steamer in a wok. Line the steamer with parchment paper liners or napa cabbage leaves.
11. Place about 1 teaspoon of shrimp filling in the middle of a wrapper.
12. Make pleats on one side of the wrapper, then fold the other side of the wrapper toward the pleated side to seal the dumpling.
13. Repeat with the remaining filling and wrappers.
14. Place the dumplings in the bamboo steamer and steam for about 5 minutes or until cooked through.
15. Place about 1 teaspoon of shrimp filling in the middle of the dumpling wrapper.
16. On one side of the wrapper, pinch the edge continuously to make pleats.
17. Fold the other side of the wrapper toward the pleated side.
18. Gently press the edges together to seal the dumpling.

Dumplings

Prep time: 2 hours | Cook time: 20 minutes| Serves 5

- 3 pounds bok choy, washed
- 1½ pounds ground pork
- ⅔ cup rice wine
- ½ cup vegetable oil
- 3 tablespoons sesame oil
- 1 tablespoon salt
- 3 tablespoons soy sauce
- ¼ teaspoon white pepper
- ⅔ cup water
- 3-4 packages dumpling wrappers
- Dipping sauce
- ½ cup soy sauce
- ½ tablespoon rice vinegar
- 1 dash hot chili sauce
- 1 green onion, sliced thinly

1. Cut the bottoms off the bok choy, and blanch it in boiling water. Transfer it immediately to ice cold water. Drain, squeeze the water out gently, and wipe it dry with paper towels. Chop the bok choy finely and place it in a large bowl.
2. Add the ground pork, rice wine, vegetable oil, sesame oil, salt, soy sauce, white pepper, and water, and mix thoroughly.
3. Line a baking sheet with parchment paper, and set it aside.
4. Place a wrapper on a clean surface and spoon about a tablespoon of filling into the center.
5. Moisten the edges with water and fold the circle over, in half.
6. Press the edges together to seal.
7. Fold the edges to get a fan-like shape (about 4 folds).
8. Arrange the dumplings on the baking sheet, not too close so they don't stick to each other.
9. To store, cover with cling wrap and freeze overnight. Transfer the frozen dumplings to another container or to Ziploc bags and replace in the freezer.
10. The dumplings may be boiled or fried. When boiled, cooked dumplings float to the top when ready. To fry, deep fry until golden brown or pan fry
11. Serve with a dipping sauce made of ½ cup of soy sauce, ½ tablespoon if rice vinegar, and a dash of chili sauce. Add green onions and mix well.

Dumplings with Peanut Sauce

Preparation time: 1 hour 30 minutes| Cooking time: 30 minutes | Makes about 40 pieces

DUMPLINGS

- 2 tablespoons vegetable oil
- 2 cloves garlic, minced
- 1 teaspoon fresh ginger, grated
- 3 green onions, sliced
- 1½ cups napa cabbage, shredded
- 4 tablespoons bamboo shoots, shredded
- 1 pound ground pork
- 2 tablespoons soya sauce
- 1 teaspoon salt
- 1 tablespoon rice wine vinegar
- ¼ teaspoon white pepper
- 2 tablespoons sesame oil
- 40-50 round dumpling wrappers
- Egg wash for sealing (1 egg beaten with 1-2 tablespoons of water)
- Peanut sauce
- ½ cup smooth organic peanut butter
- 1 cup water
- 1 tablespoon soy sauce
- 1 tablespoon hoisin sauce
- 1 teaspoon chili paste
- 1 pinch hot chili pepper flakes
- Crushed peanuts and sliced green onions for garnish

DUMPLINGS

1. Warm 2 tablespoons of vegetable oil in a wok over medium-high heat. Add the garlic and ginger. Sauté for 30 seconds. Reduce the heat to medium and add the green onions, napa cabbage, and bamboo shoots. Sauté until the vegetables are tender. Remove them from the heat and let them cool down for a few minutes.
2. Add the vegetable mixture to the raw ground pork. Mix well. Stir in the soya sauce, salt, vinegar, white pepper, and sesame oil.
3. Place 1 to 1½ teaspoons of the pork filling on one half of the wrapper. Seal the dumplings by brushing the lightly with some egg wash on the edges and folding it over. Press lightly to seal. Pleat if desired.
4. You can cook the dumplings by either steaming (preferable for better flavor) or boiling them.
5. When boiling, add them to the pot only when the water has started boiling. Let them boil for about 12 minutes.

PEANUT SAUCE

1. Combine the sauce ingredients in a blender, and mix until smooth.
2. Add some more water if necessary for the desired consistency.
3. Add enough sauce to the dumplings to coat them well. Sprinkle with crushed peanuts and green onions if desired. Serve immediately.

Damn Good Dipping Sauce

Prep time: 5 minutes | Cook time: 5 minutes| Make 3 cups

- 1 cup thin soy sauce
- ½ cup mushroom soy sauce
- ½ cup Chinkiang vinegar
- ¼ cup rice vinegar
- ½ cup sugar
- 1 tablespoon sesame oil
- 2 tablespoons chili paste
- 1 tablespoon MSG
- 1 dry chili, minced
- ¼ cup sliced scallions
- 1 tablespoon chopped cilantro

1. Add all of the ingredients in a bowl and mix until well incorporated.

Shumai

Prep time: 25 minutes | Cook time: 15 minutes| Makes at least 18 dumplings

- ½ pound pork, coarsely ground or hand-chopped
- ½ cup water chestnuts, minced
- 1 tablespoon minced ginger
- 1 teaspoon cornstarch
- 2 tablespoons oyster sauce
- 3 tablespoons thin soy sauce
- ½ egg white
- 1 pack thin yellow wonton circle wrappers
- ½ cup Damn Good Dipping Sauce

MAKING THE FILLING

1. Mix the pork, water chestnuts, ginger, cornstarch, oyster sauce, and thin soy sauce in a mixing bowl. Separately, whip a whole egg white to soft peaks, but only use half. When the pork mixture is well combined, fold in the egg white. Cover and refrigerate for 1 hour.

ASSEMBLING THE DUMPLING

2. Place 1 tablespoon of filling in wonton circle. Next, place the wrapper in one hand and begin to mold around the filling. Pleat the wrapper with your dominant hand and secure the pleats as you turn the dumpling in your grip with your non-dominant hand.
3. When all folds are secured, keep rotating the dumpling in your grip while you mold filling in the dumpling wrapper. Tap the top with your dominant index finger and middle finger, and tap the bottom with your dominant thumb. This evens out the filling.
4. Place on paper-lined tray brushed with oil to store.
5. Space out the dumplings on an oiled level in steamer with daylight between them so the steamer is not overcrowded. Steam for approximately 7 minutes and check for doneness with a meat thermometer (165°F). Remove the dumplings from the steamer and place them on a serving platter.
6. Serve with Damn Good Dipping Sauce.

Potstickers

Prep time: 25 minutes | Cook time: 10 minutes| Makes at least 18 dumplings

FOR THE DOUGH

- 1 pound all-purpose flour
- 1 tablespoon salt
- 7 ounces simmering water
- For the Filling
- ½ pound pork, coarsely ground and hand-chopped
- ½ tablespoon fermented black beans,˙ crushed into a paste
- 2 tablespoons oyster sauce
- ½ tablespoon minced garlic
- ½ tablespoon minced ginger
- 3 tablespoons soy sauce
- 2 tablespoons scallions, sliced
- 3 tablespoons water chestnuts, minced
- For the Cooking
- ½ tablespoon vegetable oil
- 12 dumplings
- 1 cup water
- ½ cup Damn Good Dipping Sauce

MAKING THE DOUGH

1. Prepare your mixer with hook attachment and set to the slowest speed.
2. Add the flour and salt to the mixer bowl then add in half of the hot water. Mix, gradually adding more water so all the flour from the bottom of the bowl is incorporated. Every environment is different, so you may need a little more water or a little less to get the correct results.
3. Mix until it forms a ball of dough that is slightly sticky, soft, and pliable. Leave the mixture in the bowl to mix for an additional 10 minutes.
4. Take the dough out of bowl, knead it slightly, wrap it with plastic wrap, and refrigerate overnight.

MAKING THE FILLING

5. Place all filling ingredients in a mixing bowl and mix until incorporated. Squeeze the mixture tightly to eliminate any air pockets. Refrigerate for 1 hour.

MAKING THE WRAPPERS

6. Cut the dough in quarters. On your work surface, work each piece of dough into a log 1 foot long by ½ inch wide without any dusting flour.
7. With a bench cutter, cut the logs into nuggets the size of the tip of your pinky, weighing half an ounce. Dust with flour, and loosely cover all with a sheet of plastic wrap to prevent drying. (At the start, intend on making one dumpling at a time. As you get faster, you can roll out 10 wrappers at a time.)
8. Dust work surface with flour, then take a nugget and roll into a ball between the palms of your hands. Place the ball on your work surface and dust it with flour.
9. Flatten the ball with heel of your palm, then take your rolling pin and dust it. Roll and flatten the perimeter of the circle. You will not roll the inner

½-inch radius of the skin; just roll back and forth along the perimeter so the edges are thinner.

10. Dust as needed to prevent sticking to your worktable. The thinness and size of the wrapper from this point is up to you and the particular dumpling. For potstickers, medium thickness, about ¹⁄16-inch thick (too thin of a skin may break when cooking), is appropriate. The diameter of the wrapper should turn out to be about a total of approximately 2 inches. You can roll out slightly larger for easier folding.
11. You now have a circle wrapper ready to be folded into a dumpling. I am right-handed, so these next steps are designed for right-handed people. Reverse for left-handed folding. Please note: I'm sure there are some small differences in the feel for folding if you are left-handed.

Soup Dumplings

Prep time: 3½ hours, rest overnight |Cook time: 8–10 minutes| Makes at least 18 dumplings

FOR THE DOUGH

- 1 pound all-purpose flour
- 1 tablespoon salt
- 7 ounces simmering water
- For the Broth Filling
- 5 pounds pork bones (or 1–2 pork or chicken bouillon cubes per gallon)
- 1 white onion, quartered
- 1 finger ginger, peeled
- 1 gallon water or to just cover bones in pot
- 2 cups oyster sauce
- 1 cup soy sauce
- ½ cup Shaoxing wine˙
- 10 pieces dried mushroom
- 2 pieces star anise
- 2 tablespoons MSG (use sparingly if using bouillon cubes)
- 2 cups cold water
- 2 cups gelatin

MAKING THE DOUGH

1. Set your mixer with hook attachment on lowest setting. Pour your flour and salt in mixer bowl, and then half of the water.
2. Mix, gradually adding more water until all the flour from the bottom of bowl is incorporated. Mix until the ball of dough is slightly sticky, soft, and pliable. Rest in the bowl to mix for an additional 10 minutes. Every environment is different, so the amount of water you need to get the correct results may vary.
3. Take the dough out of the bowl and knead slightly, then wrap with plastic wrap and rest in your refrigerator overnight.
4. Cut the dough in quarters. On your work surface, work dough into a log 1 foot long by ½ inch wide on your work surface without any dusting flour.
5. With a bench cutter, cut into nuggets the size of your pinky tip, weighing 0.5 ounce. Dust with flour and loosely cover all the dough nuggets with a sheet of plastic wrap to prevent drying. (At the start, intend on making one dumpling at a time. As you get faster, you can roll out 10 wrappers at a time.)
6. Take a nugget and roll it into a ball between the palms of your hands. Dust your work surface with flour and place the ball of dough on the surface, then dust the ball of dough with flour.
7. Flatten the ball with heel of your palm. Take your rolling pin and dust it, then roll and flatten the perimeter of the circle. Do not roll the inner ½-inch radius of the wrapper; just roll back and forth along the perimeter and stay away from the middle.
8. Dust as needed to prevent the wrappers from sticking to worktable. If you want a thin wrapper, your circle should be the same size as potsticker wrappers, maybe a touch larger, roughly 2½ inches in diameter. You can make your wrappers thicker starting with a 0.7-ounce nugget of dough. The latter is preferable for beginners to avoid breakage.
9. Even in the case where you make thinner wrappers for soup dumplings, the wrappers should really only be thin on the sides. The bottom should be left a bit thicker to prevent tearing and the tops get thicker as you fold the pleats onto each other.

FOR THE PORK AND CRAB FILLING

- 1½ pound gelatinized pork broth
- ½ pound crabmeat (buy fresh-picked blue crab or frozen)
- ½ pound ground pork, coarse grind/hand-chopped
- 3 tablespoons oyster sauce
- 1 tablespoon minced garlic
- 1 tablespoon minced ginger
- ¼ cup soy sauce
- 4 tablespoons sliced scallions
- For the Cooking
- ½ napa cabbage, sliced thin
- 1 cup Chinkiang vinegar

MAKING THE BROTH FILLING

1. There is a lot of nuance in this filling. You need to first make a broth, either using pork bones or a pork bouillon cube, then you will need to make the broth into a jelly with gelatin powder.
2. Roast the pork bones until browned, about 5 minutes. Place the bones in a pot with onion and ginger. Cover with water, then add the oyster sauce, soy sauce, Shaoxing wine, mushrooms, and star anise. Simmer for 2 hours.
3. If you're making the broth using the bouillon cubes, follow the instructions on the box, then complete the instructions below.
4. Add the MSG, then remove from the heat and strain. Add the cold water to the gelatin powder and let it bloom, about 3 to 5 minutes. Add 2 cups of bloomed gelatin to 1 quart of simmered pork broth. Stir well to fully incorporated.
5. Refrigerate overnight and the next day you should have a tight jelly. Small dice.
6. In a separate bowl, mix the crab, pork, oyster sauce, garlic, ginger, soy sauce, and scallions well.
7. Take 2 cups of the pork and crab mixture and combine with 3½ cups of the jelly, squeezing well to incorporate. Please note: the proper ratio is important.
8. Cover and refrigerate for 1 hour.

ASSEMBLING THE DUMPLINGS

1. There is one general style that is recognized for soup dumplings, although there are slightly different variants of this fold, depending on the folder and region.
2. Holding the wrapper in your non-dominant hand, place one tablespoon of filling in the middle of the wrapper. Pinch the skin with your thumb and index finger of your dominant hand and begin to create a small pleat. Secure the pleat with your dominant thumb and index finger.
3. Continuing to cradle the dumpling in your non-dominant hand, use your non-dominant thumb and index fingers to fold back each subsequent

pleat toward you.

4. Extend your dominant index finger to collect each pleat as you work circularly around the perimeter. On the last pleat, twist slightly up and connect the edges to seal.

5. Make sure that you don't pack this filling into the wrapper and squeeze the air out like the other dumplings. The contents should feel slightly loose inside. The gelatin will melt into the soup and simmer inside the dumpling, so it needs room to breathe and expand. Since the broth separates from the meat and bubbles up to the top, the amount of filling you put into each wrapper matters.

6. Steam for 6 to 7 minutes. (You can use an instant-read thermometer to check to see if the internal temperature is 165°F, but be prepared to lose a dumpling in the process.)

7. Remove the steamer basket from the base and serve the soup dumplings in the basket with Chinkiang vinegar and Chinese spoons. Slurp and enjoy.

Sui Gow (Water Dumplings)

Prep time: 25 minutes | Cook time: 10 minutes | Makes at least 18 dumplings

- ½ pound pork, coarsely ground or hand-chopped
- ½ pound 16/20 shrimp, peeled, deveined, coarsely chopped
- ½ tablespoon fermented black beans,˙ crushed into a paste
- 3 tablespoons oyster sauce
- 1½ tablespoon minced garlic
- 1½ tablespoon minced ginger
- ¼ cup soy sauce
- 4 tablespoons scallions, sliced
- ½ cup water chestnuts, minced
- 1 pack white dumpling wrappers
- 1 cup water
- ¼ cup vegetable oil
- 1 cup Damn Good Dipping Sauce

MAKING THE FILLING

1. Place pork, shrimp, fermented black beans, oyster sauce, garlic, ginger, soy sauce, scallions, and water chestnuts in a mixing bowl and mix until incorporated. Squeeze tightly to eliminate any air pockets. Cover and refrigerate for 1 hour.

ASSEMBLING THE DUMPLINGS

2. With your finger, rub water around the perimeter of the dumpling skin. Place 1¼ tablespoons filling in the skin and fold up. Gently squeeze out any air and seal. Place the finished dumplings on your sheet pan and press down a bit.

3. Set your pot of blanching water to boil and add the vegetable oil. Drop the dumplings in, but don't overcrowd the pot.

4. Cook the dumplings for approximately 4 minutes. Check for doneness, 165°F with your thermometer.

5. Strain out with a spider to a platter and serve with Damn Good Dipping Sauce.

Har Gow (Crystal Shrimp Dumplings)

Prep time: 45 minutes | Cook time: 10 minutes | Makes 16 dumplings

- For the Wrappers
- 4 ounces wheat starch
- ¾ ounce tapioca starch
- ¾ ounce potato starch
- 1 cup boiling water
- 1 ounce vegetable oil
- For the Filling
- ½ pound 16/20 shrimp, peeled, deveined, and coarsely chopped
- ⅛ cup minced bamboo shoots,˙
- ½ tablespoon salt
- 1 tablespoon MSG
- Tapioca Batter
- ¾ cup tapioca starch
- 1 cup cold water
- Cooking Ingredients
- ½ tablespoon vegetable oil (plus ½ tablespoon for each round of dumplings)
- 4 dumplings
- 3 tablespoons tapioca batter
- 1 cup water
- ½ cup abalone sauce (preferably Lee Kum Kee)

MAKING THE DOUGH

1. Prepare your mixer with paddle attachment and place on setting 2. Place the wheat starch, tapioca starch, and potato starch in mixer bowl.

2. Add the water slowly and mix until it's smooth and pliable. Add oil and knead well. Wrap in plastic wrap and rest for 30 minutes.

MAKING THE FILLING AND TAPIOCA BATTER

3. Mix shrimp with bamboo shoots, salt, and MSG. Cover and refrigerate for 1 hour.

4. Add the cold water to the starch and stir well until it has dissolved.

ASSEMBLING DUMPLINGS

5. Cut the ball of dough in half. Roll one half of the dough into a long log, approximately 1 foot long by ½ inch wide. Cut ¾-inch nuggets off the log. Press a nugget down with palm of your hand. Use a rolling pin to flatten into a thin circle.

6. Place a ½ tablespoon of filling into the circle and fold over. With practice, you can incorporate pleats into the fold. See instructions for pleated folding on pages 50–51.

COOKING THE DUMPLINGS

7. Heat an 11-inch nonstick pan on medium heat and ½ tablespoon vegetable oil. Add 4 dumplings close together in pan, then spoon 3 tablespoons of tapioca batter into the bottom of the pan.

8. Next, add 1 cup of water to pan, cover, and turn to high heat. When the water has almost evaporated from pan, remove the lid, and let the bottom crust crisp up.

9. Slide the whole crust onto a plate and serve. Repeat process as many times as needed.

10. Spoon a tablespoon of abalone sauce on each portion.

Wonton Noodle Soup

Prep time: 3½ hours | Cook time: 10 minutes | Makes 6 bowls

- For the Broth
- 2 pounds pork bones (or 2 pork bouillon)
- 1 pound fish bones (or 1 shrimp bouillon)
- 1 cup shrimp shells
- 1 gallon water
- 2 pieces star anise
- 1 cup Shaoxing wine*
- ¼ cup soy
- 2 tablespoons Chinese sugar
- 3 tablespoons MSG
- 1 tablespoon white pepper
- For the Filling
- ¼ pound shrimp, peeled, deveined, and coarsely chopped
- ½ pound pork, coarsely ground
- 2 tablespoons oyster sauce
- 3 tablespoons soy sauce
- 1 tablespoon MSG
- 1 tablespoon kosher salt
- 1 teaspoon pepper
- ½ cup sliced scallion
- 1 tablespoon peeled and minced ginger
- ½ cup minced water chestnuts
- For the Wontons
- 1 cup water
- 24 wonton wrappers
- Finishing Touches
- 2 pounds thin wonton noodles*
- 12 bok choy leaves
- 6 scallions, sliced
- 6 cilantro leaves, chopped

FOR THE BROTH

1. Combine all broth ingredients in a stockpot and simmer for 3 hours. Skim the fat off the top of the broth and then strain the broth.

MAKING THE FILLING

2. Place the shrimp, pork, oyster sauce, soy sauce, MSG, salt, pepper, scallion, ginger, and water chestnuts in a large bowl and mix until incorporated. Cover and refrigerate for 1 hour.

ASSEMBLING THE DUMPLINGS

3. Rub water around the perimeter of the wonton wrapper. Place ¾ tablespoon of the filling in the center of the wrapper, fold up, squeeze air out, and seal. Transfer your wontons to a parchment-paper-lined sheet pan brushed with oil, cover with plastic wrap, and refrigerate for 1 hour.

COOKING

4. Heat your blanching water to a boil. In separate pot, heat your broth in a pot to a simmer.
5. Place 12 wontons in the blanching water for 3 to 4 minutes and transfer to bowls; repeat for 12 remaining wontons. If the noodles are fresh, cook for 2 to 3 minutes. For dry noodles, follow the instructions on the package. Transfer to bowls.
6. Add bok choy to the blanching water for 1 minute and transfer to bowls. Ladle the broth into the bowls.
7. Garnish with scallions and cilantro. Get warm and fuzzy with 5 friends.

Raw Chocolate and Pomegranate Tart

Prep time: 15 minutes, plus 1 hour to set | Serves 8

FOR THE CRUST

- 1 cup pitted dates
- 1 cup raw walnuts
- Pinch sea salt
- FOR THE FILLING
- 1½ cups raw cacao powder
- 1 cup plus 2 tablespoons pure maple syrup
- ¾ cup coconut oil, melted
- 1 teaspoon vanilla extract
- Pinch sea salt
- ⅓ cup pomegranate seeds, plus more for topping

TO MAKE THE CRUST

1. Combine the dates, walnuts, and salt in a food processor. Process until the mixture is smooth and sticky.
2. Press the mixture into a 9-inch tart pan with a removable bottom. Place the crust in the freezer while you prepare the filling.

TO MAKE THE FILLING

1. Combine all the filling ingredients in a large bowl and mix until smooth.
2. Pour the filling into the chilled crust and smooth the top.
3. Scatter additional pomegranate seeds over the top.
4. Cover and refrigerate for at least 1 hour. Keep it chilled until ready to serve.
5. Slice and enjoy!

Dairy-Free Banana Fudge Pops

Prep time: 5 minutes, plus time to set in the freezer | Serves 6

- 1 (13-ounce) can full-fat coconut milk
- ⅓ cup raw cacao powder
- ⅔ cup raw cashews
- 2 teaspoons maca root powder (optional)
- 1 tablespoon collagen powder or unflavored gelatin powder
- Pinch sea salt
- 3 tablespoons coconut, granulated, or brown sugar
- 2 bananas, sliced

1. Combine all the ingredients in a blender and blend until smooth.
2. Pour into ice pop molds.
3. Freeze and enjoy!

Healing Hot Barley with Warming Spices

Prep time: 1 minute | Cook time: 25 minutes | Serves 4

- 3 cups water
- 1 cup barley, rinsed under running water
- ½ teaspoon ground cinnamon
- ¼ teaspoon ground turmeric
- 2 tablespoons pure maple syrup

1. In a medium saucepan, bring the water to a boil. Add the barley, reduce the heat to a simmer, and cook until the barley is soft but still a bit chewy, about 15 minutes.
2. Stir in the cinnamon, turmeric, and maple syrup. Enjoy!

Kon Tiki Bobo Meatballs

Prep time: 25 minutes | Cook time: 15 minutes | Serves 4

- Meatball ingredients
- 1 pound ground pork
- 1 cup white bread crumbs
- ½ teaspoon ground ginger
- ¼ cup white sugar
- 1 cloves garlic, minced
- Batter ingredients
- 1½ cups all-purpose flour
- 4 tablespoons white sugar
- 2 teaspoons baking soda
- 1 cup water
- 2 eggs
- Salt and pepper
- Oil for frying

1. In a mixing bowl, combine all the meatball ingredients. Season with salt and pepper.
2. Form meatballs of even sizes of about ¾ inch in diameter. Set them aside.
3. To prepare the batter, combine the flour, sugar, and baking soda. Season generously with salt and pepper. Pour the flour mixture into a shallow dish.
4. In another shallow dish, mix together the eggs and water.
5. Dip each meatball in the egg mixture and roll it in the flour mixture. Set the balls aside on a plate.
6. Heat the oil for frying, or use a deep fryer. Fry the meatballs in batches for 5 minutes. Place them on a plate lined with paper towel to drain the excess fat.
7. Serve with cocktail toothpicks and a dipping sauce like sweet and sour or cherry sauce.

Garlic Spare Ribs

Prep time: 15 minutes | Cook time: 45 minutes | Serves 4

- Water for boiling ribs
- 4 pounds spare ribs, cut apart

FOR SAUCE

- 1½ cups brown sugar
- 1½ cups water
- 5 cloves garlic
- 3½ tablespoons light soy sauce
- 1 tablespoon oyster sauce
- 1½ tablespoons dry mustard
- Spring onions, chopped (for garnish)

1. Fill a pot with water and bring it to a boil.
2. Add the spareribs, cover, and simmer until the meat is tender (about 30 minutes).
3. Remove the ribs from the broth and drain.
4. In another pot or wok, combine the ingredients for the sauce.
5. Bring it to a gentle boil, and add the spareribs.
6. Bring once again to a boil, and simmer for 10-15 minutes.
7. Serve garnished with chopped spring onion, if desired.

Cold Sesame Noodles

Prep time: 15 minutes | Cook time: 15 minutes | Serves 6 to 8 as part of a multicourse meal

- 6 ounces whole-grain spaghetti
- 2 tablespoons sesame oil, divided
- 2 tablespoons soy sauce
- 1 tablespoon rice vinegar
- 2 teaspoons brown sugar or honey
- 2 teaspoons peanut butter
- 1 carrot, julienned
- 1-inch piece ginger, peeled and minced
- 2 scallions, chopped
- 1 tablespoon sesame seeds

1. Cook the spaghetti according to the package directions for al dente. Rinse the noodles under cold water and toss in 1 tablespoon of sesame oil to prevent the noodles from sticking.
2. In a small bowl, combine the remaining 1 tablespoon of sesame oil, the soy sauce, vinegar, brown sugar, and peanut butter, mixing well.
3. Pour the mixture over the noodles then add the carrot, ginger, scallions, and sesame seeds, tossing to combine.
4. Serve chilled.

Chinese Pork Meatballs

Prep time: 15 minutes | Cook time: 15 minutes | Makes 20 meatballs

- 1 pound ground pork
- 1 tablespoon cornstarch
- 1 teaspoon minced ginger
- 3 garlic cloves, minced
- 2 teaspoons brown sugar
- 2 teaspoons soy sauce
- 1 teaspoon five-spice powder
- 2 pinches ground white pepper
- 3 tablespoons peanut oil

1. In a large bowl, combine the pork, cornstarch, ginger, garlic, brown sugar, soy sauce, five-spice powder, and pepper, and mix well.
2. Roll 1 heaping tablespoon of pork mixture into a ball and continue until all the pork mixture is used.
3. In a wok over medium heat, heat the peanut oil. Using a wok spatula, spread the oil to coat enough of the wok surface to fry about 10 meatballs at a time.
4. Lower the meatballs into the wok in batches. Cook without moving for about 2 minutes, or until the bottoms are cooked through. Use the spatula to carefully rotate the meatballs to cook on the other sides.
5. Keep rotating the meatballs gently until cooked through.

Savory Scrambled Egg And Crab Lettuce Wraps

Prep time: 15 minutes | Cook time: 15 minutes | Serves 4 to 6 as part of a multicourse meal

- 1 head lettuce
- 4 eggs, lightly beaten
- Pinch salt
- Pinch ground white pepper
- ½ teaspoon soy sauce
- 2 scallions, chopped
- 3 tablespoons peanut oil
- ½ cup diced water chestnuts
- 1 small onion, thinly sliced
- ¾ cup crabmeat

1. Wash and separate the lettuce leaves. Chill the lettuce leaves in the refrigerator until just before serving.
2. Put the beaten eggs into a medium bowl. Add the salt, pepper, soy sauce, and scallions to the eggs. Stir gently just to combine.
3. In a wok over medium-high heat, heat the peanut oil.
4. Stir-fry the water chestnuts and onion until the onion is slightly translucent.
5. Add the crabmeat to the wok, then the egg mixture, and let it sit for a moment. When the bottom of the egg is cooked through, flip, and cook on the other side.
6. Using a wok spatula, break up and scramble the egg.
7. Serve with the chilled lettuce leaves and sambal (if using).

Chinese Chicken Salad Cups

Prep time: 15 minutes | Cook time: 10 minutes | Makes 15 to 20 cups

- FOR THE CHICKEN CUPS
- 4 ounces skinless, boneless chicken tenderloins
- Salt
- Pepper
- 3 tablespoons olive oil, divided
- 15 to 20 wonton wrappers
- 1 small head romaine lettuce, shredded
- 1 carrot, julienned
- 2 scallions, chopped
- ¼ cup sliced almonds
- ¼ cup chopped fresh cilantro

FOR THE SALAD DRESSING

- 4 tablespoons apple cider vinegar
- 2 tablespoons sesame oil
- 2 tablespoons honey

1. Season the chicken tenderloins with salt and pepper. In a wok over medium heat, heat 1 tablespoon of olive oil. Add the chicken and sear on both sides until cooked through, about 1 minute per side. Remove the chicken from the wok and chop it finely.
2. Preheat the oven to 375˚F.
3. Brush each wonton wrapper on both sides with a thin layer of olive oil. Arrange the wonton wrappers in a regular-size muffin pan to form little cups.
4. Bake the wrappers for 6 minutes. Allow them to cool completely.
5. While the wrappers are baking, make the salad dressing. Combine the apple cider vinegar, sesame oil, and honey in a small bowl, and mix well.
6. In a large bowl, combine the chicken, lettuce, carrot, scallions, almonds, and cilantro with the salad dressing and toss well.
7. Fill each wonton cup with the salad and serve.

Sweet-And-Tangy Chicken Pineapple Meatballs

Prep time: 15 minutes, plus 15 minutes to chill | Cook time: 45 minutes | Serves 4

- 1 pound ground chicken
- 1 (8-ounce) can crushed pineapple, drained, juice reserved, divided
- ½ cup panko bread crumbs
- 1 large egg, lightly beaten
- 4 teaspoons cornstarch, divided
- 4 teaspoons light soy sauce, divided
- 1 tablespoon dried chives or parsley
- 1 teaspoon garlic powder
- 1 teaspoon grated fresh ginger
- 1 teaspoon onion powder
- ½ teaspoon salt
- 4 teaspoons neutral oil, divided
- 1 tablespoon honey

1. Line a rimmed baking sheet with parchment paper.
2. In a medium bowl, combine the ground chicken, ¼ cup of crushed pineapple, panko, egg, 2 teaspoons of cornstarch, 2 teaspoons of soy sauce, chives, garlic powder, ginger, onion powder, and salt. Stir vigorously for about 5 minutes until the mixture forms a paste.
3. Shape 1 heaping tablespoon of chicken mixture into a meatball and place on the lined baking sheet. Repeat with the remaining chicken mixture and roll 16 meatballs total. Cover with plastic wrap and refrigerate for at least 15 minutes, or overnight.
4. On the Instant Pot, select Sauté and preheat the pot.
5. Once hot, pour in 2 teaspoons of oil and add half the meatballs. Brown for 4 minutes, flip the meatballs, and brown for 5 minutes more. Transfer the browned meatballs to a plate. Pour in the remaining 2 teaspoons of oil and add the remaining meatballs. Brown as directed for the first batch. Transfer the browned meatballs to the plate with the first batch.
6. Add ½ cup of the reserved pineapple juice to the pot to deglaze, scraping up any browned bits from the bottom.
7. Return the meatballs to the pot and lock the lid. Program to pressure cook for 2 minutes on high pressure.
8. In a small bowl, whisk the remaining 2 teaspoons of cornstarch, 2 tablespoons of pineapple juice, remaining 2 teaspoons of soy sauce, and honey until smooth. Set aside.
9. When the timer sounds, quick release the pressure. Transfer the meatballs to a serving platter and garnish with the remaining crushed pineapple.
10. Whisk the cornstarch slurry, add it to the pot, select Sauté, and cook, stirring, for about 5 minutes until the sauce is bubbly and thickens. Drizzle some of the sauce on the meatballs and serve the remaining sauce on the side.

Chicken and Vegetable Lettuce Cups

Prep time: 15 minutes | Cook time: 15 minutes| Serves 4

- 3 teaspoons cornstarch, divided
- 1 tablespoon water, plus ¼ cup, divided
- 1 pound ground chicken
- 1 tablespoon oyster sauce
- 1 tablespoon light soy sauce
- 1 teaspoon neutral oil
- 1 medium sweet onion, chopped
- 2 garlic cloves, minced
- 2 carrots, chopped
- 1 (8-ounce) can water chestnuts, drained and diced
- 2 scallions, white and green parts, chopped
- 1 tablespoon hoisin sauce, plus ¼ cup, divided
- 1 head butter lettuce, leaves separated

1. In a small bowl, whisk 2 teaspoons of cornstarch and 1 tablespoon of water to make the slurry. Set aside.
2. In a medium bowl, mix the chicken, oyster sauce, soy sauce, and remaining 1 teaspoon of cornstarch. Set aside.
3. On the Instant Pot, select Sauté and adjust the heat to high. While the pot preheats, pour in the oil and add the onion. Stir-fry for about 3 minutes until slightly browned.
4. Add the chicken and garlic, spreading it out. Brown for 1 minute, then stir-fry for about 3 minutes until no longer pink.
5. Add the carrots and remaining ¼ cup of water to deglaze the pot, scraping up any browned bits from the bottom.
6. Lock the lid. Program to pressure cook for 1 minute on high pressure.
7. When the timer sounds, quick release the pressure. Carefully remove the lid.
8. Select Sauté, whisk the cornstarch slurry, and stir it into the pot. Add the water chestnuts, scallions, and 1 tablespoon of hoisin sauce. Cook for about 2 minutes, stirring, until the sauce thickens slightly.
9. Transfer the filling to a serving bowl and serve with lettuce cups and the remaining ¼ cup of hoisin sauce on the side.

Honey and Soy Sauce Chicken Wings

Prep time: 10 minutes, plus 30 minutes to marinate| Cook time: 25 minutes| Serves 6

- 2½ pounds chicken wing pieces
- 2 tablespoons light soy sauce
- 2 tablespoons honey
- 1 tablespoon hoisin sauce
- 1 teaspoon sesame oil
- 1 teaspoon garlic powder
- 1 teaspoon chili oil (optional)
- ½ teaspoon salt
- ½ cup water

1. In a large zip-top bag, combine the chicken wings, soy sauce, honey, hoisin sauce, sesame oil, garlic powder, chili oil (if using), and salt. Seal the bag and shake to coat. Refrigerate to marinate for 30 minutes, or overnight.
2. Place the wings, marinade, and water in the Instant Pot.
3. Lock the lid. Program to pressure cook in Poultry mode for 5 minutes on high pressure.
4. When the timer sounds, let the pressure release naturally for 5 minutes, then quick release the remaining pressure. Carefully remove the lid.
5. The wings are ready to eat, but if you want crispy skin, broil the wings in a preheated oven or in a preheated air-fryer for 1 to 2 minutes. Check frequently, so they do not burn.

Steamed Beef Meatballs

Prep time: 20 minutes, plus 10 minutes to marinate | Cook time: 15 minutes|Makes 8 meatballs

- 1 pound lean ground beef
- ½ cup chopped fresh cilantro leaves
- 4 tablespoons cold water, divided, plus 1 cup
- 4 teaspoons light soy sauce
- 1 tablespoon cornstarch
- 1 teaspoon sugar
- ¼ teaspoon salt
- ⅛ teaspoon baking soda
- ⅛ teaspoon ground white pepper
- 1 large iceberg lettuce or cabbage leaf
- 1 to 2 teaspoons Worcestershire sauce

1. In a medium bowl, combine the ground beef, cilantro, 2 tablespoons of water, soy sauce, cornstarch, sugar, salt, baking soda, and pepper. Use a wooden spoon or chopsticks to mix the ingredients, then stir in one direction for about 5 minutes until the meat becomes paste-like, adding up to 1 tablespoon more of water, if needed. Set aside to marinate for 10 minutes.
2. Pour 1 cup of water (it does not need to be cold) into the Instant Pot and place a trivet inside. Line a pressure-safe bowl with the lettuce leaf and pour in the remaining 1 tablespoon of water.
3. Divide the meat into 8 equal portions and roll each into a meatball. Place the meatballs on the lettuce leaf and place the bowl on the trivet.
4. Lock the lid. Program to pressure cook for 7 minutes on high pressure.
5. When the timer sounds, let the pressure release naturally for 5 minutes, then quick release the remaining pressure.
6. Sprinkle with Worcestershire sauce to taste and serve.

Wontons with Chicken and Pork Stock

Prep time: 55 minutes | Cook time: 15 minutes| Serves 4

8 ounces shrimp, peeled and deveined
2 teaspoons finely grated fresh ginger
8 ounces ground pork
1 cup chopped scallion, white and green parts, plus more for garnish
1 tablespoon oyster sauce
1 tablespoon light soy sauce
2 teaspoons cornstarch
2 teaspoons sesame oil
Ground white pepper
40 wonton skins
8 cups Chicken and Pork Stock

1. Chop the shrimp into the size of peas and place them in a medium bowl.
2. Add the ginger ground pork, scallion, oyster sauce, soy sauce, cornstarch, sesame oil, and ¼ teaspoon of pepper and mix well.
3. Line a rimmed baking sheet with parchment paper.
4. Open the package of wonton skins by cutting off one edge. Keep the skins in the package to avoid drying them out. Place a small bowl of water nearby.
5. Place a wonton skin on a clean, dry, flat surface with a bottom corner closest to you. Use a spoon to scoop a grape-size amount of filling and place it in the center of the wonton skin. Dip your finger into the water, wet the edges of the wonton skin, and fold up the bottom corner so it forms a triangle. Pinch the edges together firmly but without tearing the skin. Wet the three points of the triangle and bring the left and right points up to the center, folding the top point down. (Your wonton should look like a stuffed envelope.) Place it on the prepared baking sheet and repeat until all the filling is used (space the wontons apart so they don't touch).
6. Pour the stock into the Instant Pot, select Sauté, and bring to a boil.
7. Add the wontons and gently stir so they don't stick to the bottom of the pot. Cook until the wontons float, then continue to boil for 3 to 4 minutes until cooked through and the shrimp are pink. If you can't see the shrimp through the wrapper, cut one in half to check for doneness.
8. Serve the wontons in the stock with a sprinkle of scallion and a light sprinkle of pepper.

Lion Head Meatball Soup (Pork, Napa Cabbage, and Vermicelli Soup)

Prep time: 35 minutes | Cook time: 15 minutes| Serves 6

- 3 ounces (2 bundles) mung bean vermicelli
- 4 scallions, white and green parts, thinly sliced, divided
- 1 pound ground pork
- 1 cup panko or regular bread crumbs
- 2 large eggs, lightly beaten
- 2 tablespoons light soy sauce
- 1 tablespoon cornstarch
- 2 teaspoons grated fresh ginger, or 1 teaspoon ground ginger
- ¼ teaspoon salt
- Ground white pepper
- 1½ pounds (1 small head) napa cabbage, chopped into bite-size pieces
- 4 cups Chicken Stock with Ginger or store-bought chicken broth

1. In a large bowl, soak the vermicelli in water for about 15 minutes until soft. Measure ¼ cup of sliced scallion and set aside.
2. In a medium bowl, combine the ground pork, bread crumbs, eggs, remaining scallions, soy sauce, cornstarch, ginger, salt, and ½ teaspoon of pepper. Stir in one direction for about 5 minutes until the meat forms a paste. Set aside.
3. Place the cabbage in the Instant Pot. Drain the vermicelli and place it on the cabbage. Pour in the stock.
4. Divide the meat mixture into 8 equal portions and form each into a meatball. Arrange the meatballs on the vermicelli.
5. Lock the lid. Program to pressure cook for 5 minutes on high pressure. When the timer sounds, release the pressure naturally for 5 minutes, then quick release the remaining pressure.
6. Place the cabbage, vermicelli, and broth in a large serving bowl and top with the meatballs. Garnish with the reserved scallions and season with pepper.

Five-Spice Beef Shank

Prep time: 20 minutes, plus overnight to chill and marinate | Cook time: 55 minutes| Serves 6

- 1 (1½-pound) beef shank
- 8 cups water
- 4 cups beef broth or water
- ¼ cup light soy sauce
- 2 tablespoons dark soy sauce
- 2 tablespoons brown sugar
- 1 teaspoon Chinese five-spice powder
- 1 teaspoon dried Valencia orange peel (optional)
- 2 star anise pods (optional)

1. Place the beef shank in the Instant Pot and pour in the water. Select Sauté and bring the water to a boil. Parboil for 5 minutes, or until the water starts to foam. Select Cancel.
2. Rinse the shank to remove any impurities. Rinse and dry the liner before returning it to the base.
3. Return the shank to the Instant Pot, then add the broth, light and dark soy sauces, brown sugar, five-spice powder, orange peel (if using), and star anise (if using).
4. Lock the lid. Program to pressure cook for 15 minutes on high pressure
5. When the timer sounds, let the pressure release naturally for about 30 minutes.
6. Transfer the beef and sauce to a large heatproof container and let cool to room temperature. Refrigerate, covered, overnight.
7. Thinly slice the beef and serve warm or at room temperature.

Hong Kong Hot Cakes (Egg Cakes)

Prep time: 20 minutes | Cooktime: 7 minutes per cake| Makes 8 hot cakes

- 4 egg yolks (reserve the whites)
- ¾ cup sugar
- 1/3 cup butter, melted
- ¾ cup whole milk
- 1 teaspoon vanilla extract
- 1 teaspoon almond extract
- 1 cup all-purpose flour
- ½ tablespoon baking powder
- 1 pinch salt
- 6 egg whites, whipped to soft peaks
- 1 tablespoon vegetable oil
- Powdered sugar, to dust

PREPARING THE BATTER

1. When cooking this recipe, remember that the batter is at its peak for just the day. The longer it sits, the more it will start to separate and will yield a much less crispy and vibrant hot cake. If you wait too long, it will be a "not-sohot" cake. As in most situations, fresh eggs and dairy make a difference.
2. Prepare your mixer for use and attach the whisk to the mixer. Place the egg yolks in the mixer bowl and add sugar, whisking on high. If you don't have a mixer, you can just use a handheld mixer or hand-whisk.
3. Slowly add the butter and whip until smooth, then incorporate the milk, vanilla, and the almond extract.
4. In a separate mixing bowl, combine the flour, baking powder, and salt. Fold this mixture into the egg mixture gently with a spatula, just until it is incorporated. At this point, the batter should be pretty thick.
5. Next, fold in the egg whites, which will loosen up the batter slightly.

COOKING THE HOT CAKES

6. Heat pan on medium heat (or set the machine). When hot, brush oil on both sides of the pan.
7. Spoon in the batter, letting some of it overrun the holes. Close the top and place back on the heat. Heat until one side gets golden brown.
8. Flip (note: flipping is not needed if you are using an electric egg cake maker), then let other side cook for just a minute. Be patient and wait until the last second before opening the clamshell.
9. Transfer to a plate and serve. Dust with powdered sugar.

Bubble Tea

Prep time: 5 minutes | Cook time: 15 minutes| Serves 4

- 2 quarts water + 1 gallon for tapioca bubbles
- 2 cups dried oolong tea leaves
- 1 pack instant black large tapioca bubbles
- 24 ice cubes
- 8 tablespoons simple syrup
- 4 tablespoons condensed milk

FOR THE TEA AND TAPIOCA

1. Boil 2 quarts of water; once it boils, turn off the heat. Add the tea and stir. Let steep for 15 minutes and strain. Chill.
2. Boil 1 gallon of water, add the tapioca bubbles, and cook for 5 minutes. Note: There are multiple varieties in the market, each with slightly different cooking times, so follow the package instructions.
3. Strain tapioca, run under cold water for 1 minute, and reserve in cold water.
4. Fill 4 glasses with ice. Put 2 tablespoon of tapioca bubbles, 2 tablespoons of simple syrup, and 1 tablespoon of condensed milk in each glass.
5. Fill each glass with tea and stir well. Serve each glass with a big straw.

Sesame Cookies

Prep time: 15 minutes | Cook time: 25 minutes | Makes 36 cookies

- ½ cup butter
- ¾ cup shortening
- 1 teaspoon sesame oil
- ½ cup brown sugar
- ½ cup powdered sugar
- 2 eggs (1 for batter; 1 for egg wash)
- 1 teaspoon almond extract
- ½ teaspoon baking soda
- ½ teaspoon baking powder
- 1 pinch salt
- 2 cups flour
- 1 tablespoon sugar
- ½ cup sesame seeds

FOR THE DOUGH

1. Prepare your mixer with paddle attachment and set to medium. (If you don't have a mixer, add 3 hours and a workout to the recipe.)
2. Place butter, shortening, and sesame oil in mixer bowl. Start the mixer and slowly add the brown sugar, then the powdered sugar, mixing until all ingredients are well incorporated.
3. Next, add 1 egg and mix until incorporated. Then add the almond extract. In a separate bowl, mix baking soda, baking powder, salt, and flour. Set your mixer to low and add the flour mix and mix for 15 seconds until just incorporated.
4. Remove the batter from your mixer. Roll into logs, wrap in plastic wrap, and refrigerate overnight.
5. Heat your oven to 325°F.
6. Remove plastic wrap from the dough logs and cut into ½-inch portions. Roll dough portions into balls.
7. Mix 1 egg with 1 tablespoon of sugar to make your egg wash. Coat each ball of dough lightly with egg wash using a pastry brush and toss in sesame seeds.
8. Place balls of dough on a slightly oiled sheet pan and press each one slightly.
9. Bake for 15 minutes, remove from the oven, and let them rest for 10 minutes.
10. Transfer to a platter and serve with some sweet soy milk.

Lychee Custard Tart (DAN Tat)

Prep time: 2 hours + overnight (to rest dough) | Cook time: 15–20 minutes | Makes 4 tarts

FOR THE TART DOUGH

- 8 ounces all-purpose flour
- 4 ounces butter, cut into small pieces and kept cold
- 3 ounces shortening, cut into small pieces and kept cold
- 1 pinch salt
- 1 tablespoon sugar
- 3 ounces water
- Custard
- ⅓ cup sugar
- 9 egg yolks
- 3 cup cream
- 12 lychees (canned or fresh)
- Finishing Touches
- 2 tablespoons coconut flakes
- 4 scoops vanilla ice cream

FOR THE TART DOUGH

1. Pulse half the flour in a food processor with the butter and shortening. Then add the salt, sugar, water, and remaining flour and pulse three times.
2. Dust your work surface with flour and transfer dough. Work the dough slightly to make sure the fat is incorporated into the flour. Wrap in plastic wrap and rest in the refrigerator for 3 hours or overnight.
3. Once the dough has chilled, dust the work surface with flour. With a large rolling pin, flatten the dough into a smooth sheet a touch thicker than ⅛ of an inch.
4. Turn your sheet over and trace circles into the dough with a paring knife to match the size of your baking mold.
5. Mix egg and sugar together. Using a pastry brush, coat both sides of your dough circles with the sugary egg wash.

BAKING THE TART SHELL

6. Grease tart molds and place dough circles into mold. Pull the dough up slightly and crimp the edges around the edge of the molds.
7. Dock the dough: Lightly poke the tart shell with a fork to yield holes that will allow steam to escape when you bake. Return to refrigeration for 1 hour.

MAKE THE CUSTARD

8. Heat your oven to 350°F.
9. Divide the sugar between the egg yolks and cream in two separate pots. Heat the cream up to a simmer, temper (pour very slowly in increments) into the egg mixture, then whisk well.
10. Bake tarts for 2 minutes. Fill the tart with custard only half of its depth. Bake for 3 more minutes.
11. Add 3 lychees per tart and fill with custard to almost the top of the crust. The lychees will stick out halfway. Bake until done, approximately 8 minutes.
12. Remove the tarts from oven and let cool to room temperature. When serving, garnish with toasted coconut flakes and serve with a scoop of vanilla ice cream.

Chapter 13
Stir-fry Dishes

Broccoli, Yellow Peppers & Beef Stir Fry

Prep time: 5 minutes | Cook time: 5 minutes| Serves 2

- 1/2 pound beef
  1 cup broccoli
- 1/2 cup sliced yellow peppers
- 1/2 cup chopped onions
- 1 tbsp. sesame seeds
- 1 tsp. oil

1. Marinade beef in a Superfoods marinade. Stir fry drained beef in coconut oil for few minutes, add all vegetables and stir fry for 2 more minutes.
2. Add the rest of the marinade and stir fry for a minute. Serve with brown rice or quinoa.

Vegan Stir Fry

Prep time: 5 minutes | Cook time: 5 minutes| Serves 2

- 1/2 pound shiitake mushrooms
  1/2 cup Chinese celery
- 1/2 cup sliced carrots and cucumbers
- 1 Tsp. oil

1. Marinade mushrooms in a Superfoods marinade. Stir fry drained mushrooms in coconut oil for few minutes, add all other vegetables and stir fry for 2 more minutes.
2. Add the rest of the marinade and stir fry for a minute. Serve with brown rice or quinoa.

Eggplant, Chinese Celery & Peppers Stir Fry

Prep time: 5 minutes | Cook time: 5 minutes| Serves 2

- 1/2 pound cubed eggplant
  1/2 cup Chinese celery
- 1/2 cup sliced red peppers
- 1/4 cup sliced chili peppers
- 1 tsp. oil

1. Marinade eggplant in a Superfoods marinade. Stir fry drained eggplant in coconut oil for few minutes, add all vegetables and stir fry for 2 more minutes.
2. Add the rest of the marinade and stir fry for a minute. Serve with brown rice or quinoa.

Baby Corn, Snow Peas & Chicken Stir Fry

Prep time: 5 minutes | Cook time: 5 minutes| Serves 2

- 1/2 pound chicken
  1 cup baby corn
- 1/2 cup snow peas
- 1/2 cup julienned carrot
- 1/2 cup sliced mushrooms
- 1/2 cup sliced red peppers
- 1 tbsp. coconut oil

1. Marinade shrimp in a Superfoods marinade. Stir fry drained chicken in coconut oil for few minutes, add all vegetables and stir fry for 2 more minutes.
2. Add the rest of the marinade and stir fry for a minute. Serve with brown rice or quinoa.

Bamboo Shoots & Chinese Celery Stir Fry

Prep time: 5 minutes | Cook time: 5 minutes| Serves 2

- 3 cups sliced bamboo shoots
  2 cups sliced Chinese celery
- 1/2 cup sliced onions
- 1 tbsp. coconut oil

1. Stir fry bamboo shoots in coconut oil for few minutes, add Chinese celery and onions and stir fry for 2 more minutes.
2. Add the superfoods marinade and stir fry for a minute. Serve with brown rice or quinoa.

Carrot, Sesame & Spicy Beef Stir Fry

Prep time: 5 minutes | Cook time: 5 minutes| Serves 2

- 1/2 pound beef
  2 cups sliced carrots
- 1/2 cup sesame seeds
- 1/2 cup sliced onions
- 1 tbsp. coconut oil

1. Marinade shrimp in a Superfoods marinade (add 1 Tbsp. ground cumin). Stir fry beef in coconut oil for few minutes, add all vegetables and stir fry for 2 more minutes.
2. Add the rest of the marinade and stir fry for a minute. Sprinkle with sesame seeds and serve with brown rice or quinoa.

Green Pepper, Onion & BlackPeper Beef Stir Fry

Prep time: 5 minutes | Cook time: 5 minutes| Serves 2

- 1/2 pound beef stripes
  1 cup sliced green pepper
- 1/2 cup sliced celery
- 1/2 cup sliced onions
- 1 tbsp. coconut oil
- 1 tsp. black pepper

1. Marinade beef in a Superfoods marinade (add 1Tbsp. black pepper). Stir fry drained beef in coconut oil for few minutes, add all vegetables and stir fry for 2 more minutes.
2. Add the rest of the marinade and stir fry for a minute. Serve with brown rice or quinoa.

String Beans, Onion & Beef Stir Fry

Prep time: 5 minutes | Cook time: 5 minutes| Serves 2

- 1/2 pound beef
  2 cups sliced string onion
- 1/2 cup sliced onions
- 1 red chili pepper
- 1 Tbsp. coconut oil

1. Marinade shrimp in a Superfoods marinade. Stir fry drained shrimp in coconut oil for few minutes, add all vegetables and stir fry for 2 more minutes.
2. Add the rest of the marinade and stir fry for a minute. Serve with brown rice or quinoa.

Bitter Gourd & Minced Meat Stir Fry

Prep time: 5 minutes | Cook time: 5 minutes| Serves 2

- 1/2 pound minced beef
  2 cups sliced bitter gourd
- 1/2 cup sprouts
- 1/2 cup sliced onions
- 1 Tbsp. coconut oil

1. Marinade minced beef in a Superfoods marinade. Stir fry drained minced beef in coconut oil for few minutes, add all vegetables and stir fry for 2 more minutes.
2. Add the rest of the marinade and stir fry for a minute. Serve with brown rice or quinoa.

Snow Peas, Chicken & Asparagus Stir Fry

Prep time: 5 minutes | Cook time: 5 minutes| Serves 2

- 1/2 pound chicken
  2 cups sliced snow peas
- 1/2 cup sliced asparagus
- 1/2 cup julienned carrots
- 1 Tbsp. coconut oil

1. Marinade chicken in a Superfoods marinade. Stir fry drained chicken in coconut oil for few minutes, add all vegetables and stir fry for 2 more minutes.
2. Add the rest of the marinade and stir fry for a minute. Serve with brown rice or quinoa.

Green Peas, Pork, Onions & Cilntro Stir Fry

Prep time: 5 minutes | Cook time: 5 minutes| Serves 2

- 1/2 pound pork
  1 cup Green peas
- 1 cup sliced onions
- 1/4 cup cilantro
- 1 Tbsp. coconut oil

1. Marinade pork in a Superfoods marinade. Stir fry drained pork and green peas in coconut oil for few minutes, add onions and stir fry for 2 more minutes.
2. Add the rest of the marinade and stir fry for a minute. Serve with brown rice or quinoa.

Sechuan Beef, Celery, Carrot & Chili Sauce Stir Fry

Prep time: 5 minutes | Cook time: 5 minutes| Serves 2

- 1/2 pound beef
  1 cup sliced celery
- 1/2 cup sliced carrot
- 1 tbsp. coconut oil

1. Marinade beef in a Superfoods marinade and chili sauce. Stir fry drained beef in coconut oil for few minutes, add celery and carrot and stir fry for 2 more minutes.
2. Add the rest of the marinade and stir fry for a minute. Serve with brown rice or quinoa.

Asparagus, Yellow Peppers & Tomato Stir Fry

Prep time: 5 minutes | Cook time: 5 minutes| Serves 2

- 1/2 pound asparagus
  1 cup sliced yellow peppers
- 1 cup chopped tomato
- 1 tbsp. coconut oil

1. Marinade asparagus in a Superfoods marinade. Stir fry drained asparagus in coconut oil for 7-8 minutes, add peppers and tomato and stir fry for 2 more minutes.
2. Add the rest of the marinade and stir fry for a minute. Serve with brown rice or quinoa.

Bok Choy, Almonds, Onions & Sesame Stir Fry

Prep time: 5 minutes | Cook time: 5 minutes| Serves 2

- 1/2 pound bok choy
  1 + ½ cup sliced onions
- 3 tbsp. almond slices
- 1 tbsp. sesame seeds
- 1 tbsp. coconut oil

1. Marinade bok choy in a Superfoods marinade. Stir fry drained bok choy and onions in coconut oil for few minutes, add almond and sesame seeds and stir fry for 2 more minutes.
2. Add the rest of the marinade and stir fry for a minute. Serve with brown rice or quinoa.

Broccoli, Turkey Breast & Carrots Stir Fry

Prep time: 5 minutes | Cook time: 5 minutes| Serves 2

- 1/2 pound turkey breast, cubed
  1 cup sliced broccoli
- 3/4 cup sliced carrots
- 1 Tbsp. coconut oil

1. Marinade turkey in a Superfoods marinade. Stir fry drained turkey in coconut oil for few minutes, add carrot and broccoli and stir fry for 2 more minutes.
2. Add the rest of the marinade and stir fry for a minute. Serve with brown rice or quinoa.

Broccolini, Zucchini, Tomatoes & Onions Stir Fry

Prep time: 5 minutes | Cook time: 5 minutes| Serves 2

- 1/2 pound broccolini
  1 cup sliced zucchini
- 3/4 cup sliced onions
- 3/4 cup chopped tomato
- 1 tbsp. coconut oil

1. Marinade broccolini in a Superfoods marinade. Stir fry drained broccolini in coconut oil for few minutes, add zucchini and onions and stir fry for 2 more minutes.
2. Add tomatoes and the rest of the marinade and stir fry for a minute. Serve with brown rice or quinoa.

Cabbage, Green Onions & Chicken Stir Fry

Prep time: 5 minutes | Cook time: 5 minutes| Serves 2

- 1/2 pound sliced chicken
  1 cup sliced cabbage (or Chinese Napa cabbage)
- 1/2 cup sliced celery
- 2 sliced green onions
- 1/2 cup cashews
- 1 Tsp. oil

1. Marinade chicken in a Superfoods marinade. Stir fry drained chicken in coconut oil for few minutes, add all vegetables and stir fry for 2 more minutes.
2. Add the rest of the marinade and stir fry for a minute. Serve with brown rice or quinoa.

Naachi Bokum - Spicy Octopus Zucchini Stir Fry

Prep time: 5 minutes | Cook time: 5 minutes| Serves 2

- 1/2 pound cubed octopus
  1 cup sliced zucchini
- 1/2 cup sliced carrot
- 2 sliced green onions
- 1/2 cup sliced celery
- 1 Tsp. oil and 1 tsp. chili

1. Marinade octopus in a Superfoods marinade and chili. Stir fry drained octopus in coconut oil for few minutes, add all vegetables and stir fry for 2 more minutes.
2. Add the rest of the marinade and stir fry for a minute. Serve with brown rice or quinoa.

Chapter 14
Salads and Cold Appetizers

Smacked Cucumber Salad

Prep time: 10 minutes, plus 20 minutes to rest | Cook time: 5 minutes | Serves 4

- 2 large English cucumbers
- 1 tablespoon sea salt
- 4 garlic cloves, minced
- 3 tablespoons black vinegar
- 2 teaspoons Chinese light soy sauce
- 2 teaspoons sesame oil
- 1½ teaspoons granulated sugar
- 1 tablespoon Sichuan Chili Oil or store-bought chili oil
- ½ cup fresh cilantro, cut into 2-inch lengths

1. Trim the ends off the cucumbers and lay them on a cutting board. Smack the cucumbers firmly with the flat side of a chef's knife, working from one end of the cucumber to the other, until the cucumbers crack. Split the smacked cucumbers in half lengthwise. Lay each half flat-side up. Cut the cucumbers diagonally into ½-inch-thick, 2-inch-long slices.
2. In a medium bowl, toss the cucumber and salt together until thoroughly combined and let them rest for 20 minutes.
3. Squeeze out as much juice as possible from the cucumber (discard the cucumber juice). Transfer the cucumber to a clean medium bowl.
4. Add the garlic, vinegar, soy sauce, sesame oil, sugar, chili oil, and cilantro to the bowl. Mix everything together.
5. For the best flavor, refrigerate the salad until you serve it.

Mixed Rainbow Vegetable Salad

Prep time: 10 minutes | Cook time: 5 minutes | Serves 4

- 3 cups lightly packed frisée, cut into 2-inch segments
- ½ red bell pepper, cut into bite-size pieces
- ½ yellow bell pepper, cut into bite-size pieces
- 1 cup (1¾ oz / 50g) lightly packed bite-size pieces red cabbage
- 6 red radishes, thinly sliced
- ¼ large English cucumber, thinly sliced
- ¼ cup white rice vinegar
- 2 tablespoons Chinese light soy sauce
- 1 tablespoon vegetarian oyster sauce
- 1 tablespoon granulated sugar
- ½ teaspoon sea salt
- 1 teaspoon sesame oil
- ¼ cup roasted peanuts (any papery skins removed)

1. In a large salad bowl, combine the frisée, bell pepper, cabbage, radish, and cucumber.
2. In a small bowl, mix the rice vinegar, soy sauce, vegetarian oyster sauce, sugar, salt, and sesame oil together. Stir with chopsticks to dissolve the sugar and salt.
3. Add the peanuts to the vegetables. Pour the dressing into the bowl. Mix together and serve immediately.

Wood Ear Mushroom Salad

Prep time: 10 minutes, plus 2 to 4 hours to rehydrate | Cook time: 5 minutes | Serves 4

- ¾ cup (¾ oz / 21g) dried wood ear mushrooms, soaked in cool water for 2 to 4 hours
- ¼ cup thinly sliced red onion
- 1 fresh bird's eye chili, sliced into thin rings
- 2 garlic cloves, minced
- 2 tablespoons Chinese light soy sauce
- 1 tablespoon black vinegar
- 1 teaspoon sesame oil
- ¾ teaspoon granulated sugar
- ⅓ cup roughly chopped fresh cilantro

1. Set up a bowl of cold water. Bring a medium pot of water to a boil over high heat.
2. Rinse the soaked wood ears and discard the tough roots. Add the mushrooms to the boiling water and cook for 5 minutes. Transfer the mushrooms to the cold water to cool, then drain thoroughly.
3. Using your hands, tear the larger pieces of mushrooms into bite-size pieces.
4. In a medium bowl, combine the wood ears, onion, chili, garlic, soy sauce, vinegar, sesame oil, sugar, and cilantro. For the best flavor, refrigerate the salad until you serve it.

Easy Asparagus Salad

Prep time: 5 minutes | Cook time: 5 minutes | Serves 4

- 1 pound (454g) asparagus
- 1 tablespoon canola oil
- 1½ teaspoons sea salt, divided
- 2 garlic cloves, minced
- 1 teaspoon sesame oil
- ½ teaspoon toasted sesame seeds (optional)

1. Snap off the tough ends of the asparagus spears. Cut the asparagus diagonally into 2-inch-long pieces.
2. Bring a medium pot of water to a boil over high heat. Add the canola oil and 1 teaspoon of salt. Add the asparagus and blanch for about 2 minutes, or until it is just tender.
3. Drain the asparagus in a colander and let it cool to room temperature.
4. Transfer the cooled asparagus to a medium bowl and toss it with the garlic, sesame oil, and remaining ½ teaspoon of salt.
5. Sprinkle with toasted sesame seeds (if using) and serve.

Assorted Vegetarian Delicacies

Prep time: 10 minutes, plus 8 to 16 hours to soak and to marinate|Cook time: 20 minutes| Serves 6

- 8 medium dried shiitake mushrooms (¾ oz / 20g), soaked in cool water for 2 hours or up to overnight
- ⅓ cup (⅓ oz / 9g) dried wood ear mushrooms, soaked in cool water for 2 to 4 hours
- ½ cup (¾ oz / 20g) dried lily flowers, soaked in warm water for 30 minutes
- 1 or 2 dried bean curd sticks (1oz / 30g), soaked in cool water for 4 to 6 hours
- 1 cup water
- 3 tablespoons granulated sugar
- 2 tablespoons Chinese light soy sauce
- 1 tablespoon dark soy sauce
- 1 teaspoon sea salt
- 4 tablespoons canola oil, divided
- 2½ cups (7oz / 200g) 1-inch cubed Steamed Seitan or store-bought Chinese steamed seitan (kao fu)
- 2 whole star anise
- 1 cinnamon stick
- ½ cup roasted peanuts (any papery skins removed)
- ¼ cup thinly sliced canned bamboo shoots, drained
- 2 tablespoons sesame oil

1. Scoop out the rehydrated shiitakes, wood ears, lily flowers, and bean curd sticks from their respective bowls. Squeeze out the water. Reserve 1 cup of the shiitake soaking water.
2. Discard the tough ends from both types of mushroom and the lily flowers. Thinly slice the shiitake and cut the bean curd sticks into 1-inch segments at an angle.
3. In a medium bowl, combine the water, shiitake soaking water, sugar, light soy sauce, dark soy sauce, and salt. Set the sauce aside.
4. In a wok or skillet with a lid, heat 2 tablespoons of canola oil over medium-high heat until hot. Add the seitan cubes and stir for 2 minutes. Remove them and set them aside on a plate, leaving any extra oil in the pan.
5. Add the remaining 2 tablespoons of canola oil to the pan, then add the shiitake, star anise, and cinnamon stick and stir for 1 minute to release the spices' fragrance. Add the wood ear mushroom, lily flowers, bean curd sticks, peanuts, and bamboo shoots and stir for 2 minutes.
6. Add the seitan and the sauce to the pan and mix. Cover the pan, reduce the heat to medium-low, and simmer everything for 15 minutes, or until most of the sauce has reduced. If there is still a lot of sauce, uncover the pan and cook for a few more minutes. Remove the mixture from the heat and drizzle it with the sesame oil.
7. Transfer the mixture to a sealed container and refrigerate it for 4 hours, or until well chilled, before eating.

Steamed Eggplant In Garlic-Sesame Sauce

Prep time: 20 minutes, plus 10 minutes to cool|Cook time: 15 minutes| Serves 6

- ¼ cup distilled white vinegar
- 1 medium globe eggplant (1¼ lb / 567g) or 2 Italian eggplants
- 3 tablespoons Chinese sesame paste
- 3 tablespoons water
- 1¼ teaspoons sea salt
- 6 garlic cloves, peeled
- 2 teaspoons sesame oil
- 2 tablespoons chopped fresh cilantro
- SPECIAL EQUIPMENT:
- Flat-bottomed stainless steel or bamboo steamer with a large pot

1. Fill a large bowl halfway with water and add the white vinegar. Peel the eggplant, cut it into ½-inch-thick slices, and immediately submerge the slices in the water to prevent browning.
2. Heat a pot of water with a steamer on top over high heat. When the pot is steaming, reduce the heat to medium and place the eggplant in the steamer. Shingle the eggplant slices into the steamer, overlapping them slightly to allow steam to come in between. Steam the eggplant for 10 minutes, or until tender. Remove the eggplant from the steamer and let it cool.
3. Meanwhile, in a small bowl, combine the sesame paste, water, and salt and stir into a smooth sauce. Using a small food processor or a mortar and pestle, thoroughly mash the garlic into a paste.
4. Squeeze any excess water out of the eggplant and use your hands to pull it into small, bite-size chunks. In a medium bowl, combine the eggplant, sesame sauce, mashed garlic, sesame oil, and cilantro and stir well.
5. Serve as an appetizer or side dish.

Boiled Young Soybeans

Prep time: 5 minutes, plus 2 hours to marinate|Cook time: 25 minutes| Serves 6

- 3 whole star anise
- 2 teaspoons red Sichuan peppercorns
- 3 bay leaves
- 1½ tablespoons sea salt
- 4 cups water

1. In a medium pot, toast the star anise, Sichuan peppercorns, bay leaves, and salt over medium-low heat for 3 minutes, or until fragrant, stirring frequently to make sure the spices do not burn.
2. Pour the water into the pot with the spices, then bring it to a boil over high heat. Once the water has boiled, reduce the heat to medium-low and simmer the spices for 5 minutes.
3. Meanwhile, using a pair of scissors, cut off both ends of the edamame pods. (This will help the soybeans absorb flavor.) Add the soybeans to the pot, increase the heat to high, and bring the liquid to a boil again. Then reduce the heat to medium and simmer the soybeans for 4 minutes.
4. Remove the pot from the heat. Keep the soybeans in the brine to absorb its flavor while the liquid cools to room temperature. Remove the soybeans from the brine to serve.

Taiwan-Style Pickled Cabbage

Prep time: 10 minutes, plus 1 hour to rest and pickle| Serves 6

- ½ medium Taiwanese flat cabbage (1lb 12oz / 795g) or 1 small green cabbage
- 1 medium carrot, thinly julienned
- 1 tablespoon sea salt
- 2 fresh bird's eye chilies
- ½ cup granulated sugar
- ½ cup white rice vinegar
- 4 garlic cloves, sliced

1. Remove the core of the cabbage, then cut along the cabbage midribs to split the thick ribs in half. Tear the leaves into large bite-size pieces.
2. In a large bowl, toss the cabbage pieces and the carrot with the salt. Gently massage the vegetables with your hands for 2 minutes to work in the salt, then let them sit for 30 minutes.
3. Once the vegetables have released their juices, transfer the cabbage and carrots to a colander to drain, then rinse off the remaining salt. Squeeze the vegetables to remove as much liquid as possible.
4. Put the vegetables and the dressing into a large, airtight glass container. Seal the container and shake it to mix the vegetables and the dressing together. Refrigerate the mixture for at least 30 minutes.
5. Transfer your desired amount of the pickled vegetables onto a plate and serve it cold. To store the remaining pickled cabbage, leave it in the sealed container in the refrigerator for up to 1 week.

Sour and Spicy Pickled Daikon

Prep time: 10 minutes, plus 1 day and 30 minutes to rest and pickle| Serves 6

- 1 daikon radish (1lb 12oz /795g)
- 1 tablespoon sea salt
- 1½ cups water
- 1 cup distilled white vinegar
- ¼ cup granulated sugar
- 1 (1-inch) piece fresh ginger, thinly sliced
- 4 garlic cloves, thinly sliced
- 4 fresh bird's eye chilies, cut into small rings

1. Peel and cut the daikon radish into 2-inch-long strips ¼ inch thick and transfer them to a large bowl.
2. Sprinkle the salt on the daikon and use your hands to mix thoroughly. Let the daikon rest for 30 minutes.
3. In a medium bowl, mix the water, vinegar, and sugar until well combined.
4. Drain the daikon in a colander, then put it into a clean large bowl. Add the ginger, garlic, and chili and mix everything well, then transfer the mixture to a large glass jar with a lid.
5. Pour the pickling liquid into the jar, making sure it covers the daikon. Close the jar and let the daikon pickle for 1 day in the refrigerator before eating.
6. Remove some daikon from the jar and serve as an appetizer. You can keep the rest submerged in the pickling liquid and store it in the refrigerator for up to 2 weeks.

Qianlong Cabbage

Prep time: 15 minutes | Cook time: 5 minutes| Serves 4

- 3 tablespoons Chinese sesame paste
- 2 tablespoons granulated sugar
- 2 tablespoons black vinegar
- 1 teaspoon sesame oil
- ½ teaspoon dark soy sauce
- ¼ teaspoon sea salt
- 1 tablespoon maple syrup
- 5 cups (9oz / 250g) tightly packed napa cabbage leaves, inner yellow leaves only (no midribs)
- 1 tablespoon toasted white sesame seeds, plus more for garnish

1. In a large bowl, mix the sesame paste, sugar, black vinegar, sesame oil, dark soy sauce, salt, and maple syrup together. The mixture should be thick and stick to the spoon.
2. Tear the cabbage leaves into large bite-size pieces and add them to the bowl. Mix the cabbage and the sauce together until all the leaves are coated. Mix in the sesame seeds.
3. Stack the cabbage in a small pile on a plate and garnish them with more sesame seeds. Serve immediately.

Appendix 1 Measurement Conversion Chart

Volume Equivalents (Dry)	
US STANDARD	**METRIC (APPROXIMATE)**
1/8 teaspoon	0.5 mL
1/4 teaspoon	1 mL
1/2 teaspoon	2 mL
3/4 teaspoon	4 mL
1 teaspoon	5 mL
1 tablespoon	15 mL
1/4 cup	59 mL
1/2 cup	118 mL
3/4 cup	177 mL
1 cup	235 mL
2 cups	475 mL
3 cups	700 mL
4 cups	1 L

Volume Equivalents (Liquid)		
US STANDARD	**US STANDARD (OUNCES)**	**METRIC (APPROXIMATE)**
2 tablespoons	1 fl.oz.	30 mL
1/4 cup	2 fl.oz.	60 mL
1/2 cup	4 fl.oz.	120 mL
1 cup	8 fl.oz.	240 mL
1 1/2 cup	12 fl.oz.	355 mL
2 cups or 1 pint	16 fl.oz.	475 mL
4 cups or 1 quart	32 fl.oz.	1 L
1 gallon	128 fl.oz.	4 L

Temperatures Equivalents	
FAHRENHEIT(F)	**CELSIUS(C) APPROXIMATE)**
225 °F	107 °C
250 °F	120 ° °C
275 °F	135 °C
300 °F	150 °C
325 °F	160 °C
350 °F	180 °C
375 °F	190 °C
400 °F	205 °C
425 °F	220 °C
450 °F	235 °C
475 °F	245 °C
500 °F	260 °C

Weight Equivalents	
US STANDARD	**METRIC (APPROXIMATE)**
1 ounce	28 g
2 ounces	57 g
5 ounces	142 g
10 ounces	284 g
15 ounces	425 g
16 ounces (1 pound)	455 g
1.5 pounds	680 g
2 pounds	907 g

Appendix 2 The Dirty Dozen and Clean Fifteen

The Environmental Working Group (EWG) is a nonprofit, nonpartisan organization dedicated to protecting human health and the environment Its mission is to empower people to live healthier lives in a healthier environment. This organization publishes an annual list of the twelve kinds of produce, in sequence, that have the highest amount of pesticide residue-the Dirty Dozen-as well as a list of the fifteen kinds of produce that have the least amount of pesticide residue-the Clean Fifteen.

THE DIRTY DOZEN	
The 2016 Dirty Dozen includes the following produce. These are considered among the year's most important produce to buy organic:	
Strawberries	Spinach
Apples	Tomatoes
Nectarines	Bell peppers
Peaches	Cherry tomatoes
Celery	Cucumbers
Grapes	Kale/collard greens
Cherries	Hot peppers

The Dirty Dozen list contains two additional itemskale/collard greens and hot peppers-because they tend to contain trace levels of highly hazardous pesticides.

THE CLEAN FIFTEEN	
The least critical to buy organically are the Clean Fifteen list. The following are on the 2016 list:	
Avocados	Papayas
Corn	Kiw
Pineapples	Eggplant
Cabbage	Honeydew
Sweet peas	Grapefruit
Onions	Cantaloupe
Asparagus	Cauliflower
Mangos	

Some of the sweet corn sold in the United States are made from genetically engineered (GE) seedstock. Buy organic varieties of these crops to avoid GE produce.

Appendix 3 Index

PARK HOU

Printed in Great Britain
by Amazon

13797503R00059